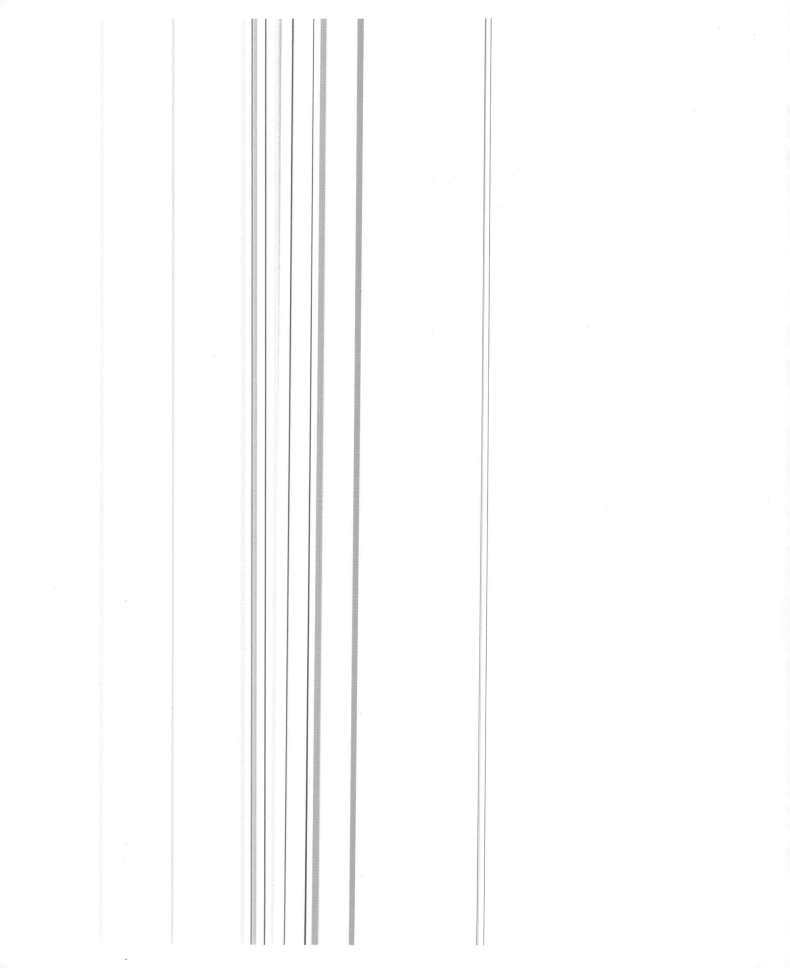

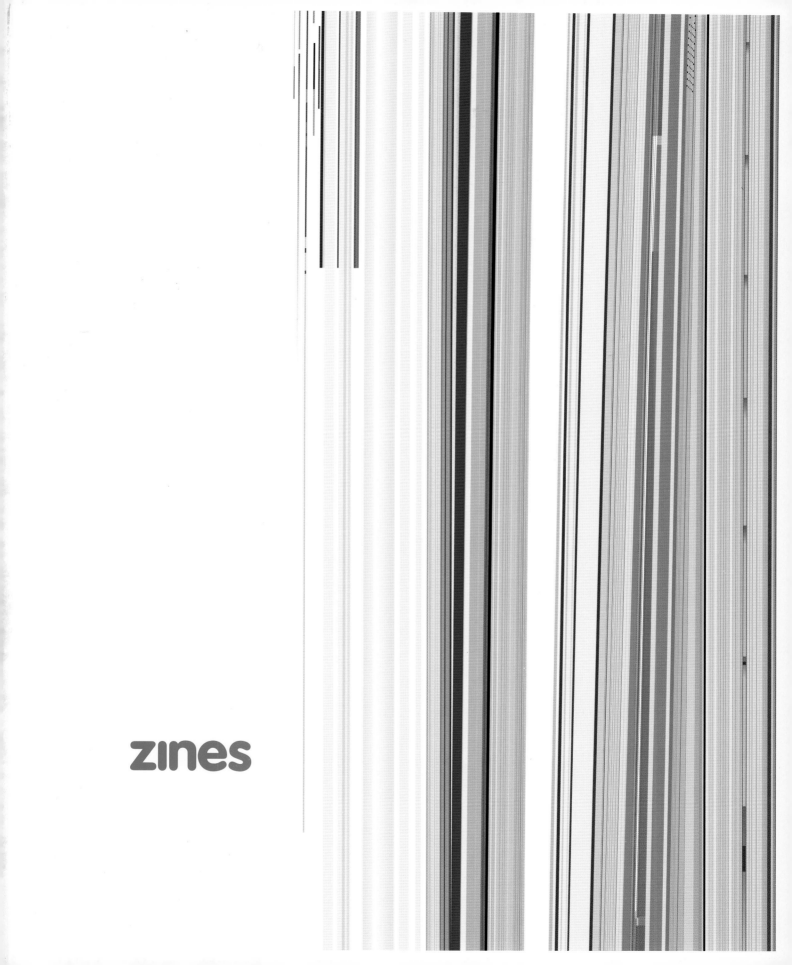

zines

First Published in 2001 by
Booth-Clibborn Editions
12 Percy Street
London
W1T 1DW
www.booth-clibborn.com

Editor_Liz Farrelly
Design_Mike Dorrian_David Recchia

Photography_emmerichwebb

The information in this book is based on
material supplied to Booth-Clibborn
Editions Limited by the entrants. While
every effort has been made to ensure its
accuracy, Booth-Clibborn Editions Limited
does not under any circumstances accept
responsibility for any errors or omissions.

A Cataloguing-in-Publication record for
this book is available from the Publisher.

ISBN 1-86154-224-0

Printed by DNP in Hong Kong

thank you
Ric Blackshaw_Chloe Erlam_Gregg
Virostek_Igor Emmerich_Nicola Webb and
Olive_The Beta Band_Fire_Magma_Todd
James_Ryan McGinness_Misha
Hollenbach_Dave the Chimp_Anja Lutz_
Green Lady_Hitch_Matthew McCarthy_
Hugh Somerville_Toko_Ann-Marie Payne_
anand zenz_Randy Wood_Jason Creed_
Jake Tilson_Stephen Baker_Andrew
McGovern_Liz Wakefield_Hilary Judd_
Toby Tripp_Vortex_Kyn Taylor_Lynn Peril_
Carl Ison_Lee Curtis_Stuart Williams_Chris
North_Seb Pizzutto_Vic Salmon_Carl
Thomas_Jessica Chamberlen_Katy
Langdown_Debi Warman_Sally Robson_
Lisa Meiller_Sue Howells_Steve Frost_The
Boy Lucas and John Coe_Jeanette Ordas_
Dan Wu_Scott Andrew Snyder_James
Jarvis_Ron Turner_Presley_Neil Boorman_
Michael Oliveira-Salac_Kira Jolliffe_
Rick Pinchera_Keffo_Mona Weiner_
Jim Munroe_Stephen Stewart_Molly M.
Cannon and Tara J. McCaw_John Ronsen
_Mimi Zeiger_David Lester_Ensa Humano
Eric Braün Alex Smith_Chris Love_Juliette
Torrez_Ninj_Danny_Marieke and Cindy_
PHK International_The Team_Ian Sen_
Peter Maybury_Mark Pawson_Roger Sabin
_Peter Pavement_Flight Club_Tim Lewis_
Athony Burrill_Cactus_Johnny Brewton_
Amanda Waring_RYK@MBD_Sally Hems–
Hiro Sugiyama_ Masanobu Sugatsuke_
Tom Snyders_David Lester_Paul Higgins_
Fishburn-Hedges

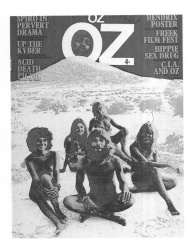

OZ_30
JIM ANDERSON

COVER PHOTO **KARL FERRIS**
FORMAT **230mm x 300mm**
MATERIAL **MIXED STOCK**
TIME_PLACE **1971_UK**
PUBLISHER **OZ PUBLICATIONS INK**

OZ_44
JIM ANDERSON

COVER PHOTO **GINGER GORDON**
FORMAT **210mm x 300mm**
MATERIAL **MIXED STOCK**
TIME_PLACE **1972_UK**
PUBLISHER **OZ PUBLICATIONS INK**

SNIFFIN GLUE_12
MARK PERRY

COVER PHOTO **ERICA ECHENBURG**
FORMAT **210mm x 297mm**
MATERIAL **PHOTOCOPIES**
TIME_PLACE **1977_UK**

Hello and welcome to zine world...

Our aim with this book is to highlight the graphic language of zines, small press and independent publications, and present it to a larger audience than may usually get to see such underground editions. Culled from travels around the globe, we think we've found some choice examples; but we're not claiming to offer a comprehensive overview, as the world of self-publishing is huge and varied, shifts like quick sand and has a long and intricate history, which a number of academic scholars are in the process of unravelling. Instead, we've set out to take the pulse of this uniquely personal form of graphic expression at a time in its evolution when some say, the zine is dead, mutated by the internet into home-pages, chat-sites and e-zines. What we've found however is a vast wealth of creativity; where form is constantly being reinvented; tampered with by lawless "amateurs" (practitioners who didn't train at art school, no less). We think that's just great, we love it in fact. Alongside the enthusiasts are other makers who unashamedly revel in the spontaneity of drawing or photocopying and in exploring the tactile qualities of many inks on various papers.

We've allowed ourselves to travel back in time a little, as some of our favourites from days past are still benchmarks within the zine-ing community. But we've tried not to include defunct titles. Many great zines have grown into magazines proper; Bust, Punk Planet, Maximumrocknroll, Hip Mama for instance, or faded away. Others are "resting" and we've taken the liberty of including some of those. As for the foundation stones of zinedom, you won't necessarily see them here either; Punk, i-D, Duplex Planet, Vague, Search and Destroy, because they're well documented elsewhere.

We've tried to include examples from across the genres of zine publishing, alongside a host of one-offs from regular self-publishers who are active right now. A quick trawl of zines currently on offer makes mainstream magazine racks look boring and restrictive. So check out zines on; obsolete objects, 60s, 70s and 80s collectables, sci-fi, goth and gore, soccer, poetry, architecture, organic food, eight-track tapes, graffiti, clip art, McJobs, direct action, consumer boycotts, babycare, D-I-Y culture, thrifting, exotic dancing, skateboarding...

...the list is too big.

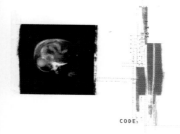

MAXIMUN SPEED_7

COVER PHOTO **GEORGE BODNER**
FORMAT **210mm x 297mm**
MATERIAL **PHOTOCOPIES**
TIME_PLACE **1979_UK**

CODE 395_ANOTHER TEMPORARY RELEASE
IAN SEN_PETER MAYBURY_
JENI GLASGOW_JOHNNY MOY

FORMAT **255mm x 255mm**
MATERIAL **UNCOATED PAPER**
TIME_PLACE **1995_IRELAND**

PHASIS_2
JUSTIN HAMMOND_
MARTIN LESANTO SMITH

FORMAT **145mm x 210mm**
MATERIAL **CARTRIDGE PAPER**
TIME_PLACE **1996_UK**

Most importantly, where do you find these wonderful objects? As **Factsheet 5**, the original meta-zine (i.e. publishes reviews on every genre of zine) is on sabatical, try these other worthy publications.
ByPass, PO Box 2927, Brighton, Sussex, BN1 3SX, UK
bypass@bedsit.freeserve.co.uk
www.bypass-zine.co.uk

Broken Pencil, PO Box 203, Stn. P, Toronto, ON, M5S 2S7, Canada
editor@brokenpencil.com
www.brokenpencil.com

Zine Guide, PO Box 5467, Evanston, IL 60204, USA
zineguide@interaccess.com

Other places to pick up zines, world-wide, try; the Last Chance Saloon, Rough Trade, Disinfotainment, ICA, Magma, Tower Records, Gosh Comics, Helter Skelter, all in London.
Edge World Records in Brighton.
Arnofini in Bristol.
Collette in Paris.
Galerie Lambiek in Amsterdam.
Printed Matter, Ink on A, See Hear, Blue Stocking Women's Bookshop in New York City.
Aquarius Records, Dog-eared Books in San Francisco.
Houston in Seattle and Tokyo.
Black Sheep Books in Vancouver.
There are others, these are just some of our favourite places...

How to use this book

The main body of this book is visual. We want you to see just how graphically innovative these publications are, so we've pulled out favourite images and played with them. Up at the front of the book is information about the zines; dimensions, materials and dates. We've selected writings from the publications and printed taster samples; sadly there just isn't space for complete articles, but many of the existing books on zines present written content very comprehensively. Also up front are quotes from the makers themselves, either as they appear in editorials and articles, or via e-mail and telephone conversations. And, if we only had the object to go on, we've added a little more description of its form and content. Then, at the back of the book, is a bibliography; it's not exhaustive, but there's enough informed and entertaining writing there to keep any budding zine fan busy for a good while.

We've stretched our rules a little on this spread, to show a few seminal influences and some progressive steps in the evolution of one genre. Here's some past gems in the music zines category, just to whet your appetite.

001z_002z

ATLAS_3_4
JAKE TILSON

DESIGN **ATLAS**
FORMAT **210mm x 285mm**
MATERIAL **MIXED STOCK**
TIME_PLACE **1987-1993_UK**
PUBLISHER **THE WOOLLEY DALE PRESS_ATLAS**

www.areaatlas.com
info@areaatlas.com

Atlas is a collation of artists' contributions in many media. Issue 3, the Audience Participation issue, includes; a 20-page bind it yourself book, a collage kit in a plastic bag, a Neil Jeffries construction, an issue of **Spy** by John Watson and drawings by Dillwyn Smith, Therese Oulton and Helen Wilde. Issue 4 includes contributions from; Lee Ranaldo of Sonic Youth, Richard Wentworth, Howard A. Bern, Maria Chevska, Steve Reich, Suzanne Evans and an **Atlas** alphabet by Jake Tilson. And despite a hiatus, it's still ongoing...

Quote Jake Tilson: **Atlas** 5 is an "active" box, but I don't think the ideas contained in it will become another magazine; they may become a website. The entire publishing landscape has changed so dramatically over the last seven years that to produce a printed version of **Atlas** 5 would seem out of place. My published works, since the last books of the early 1990s, have been audio, video and web-based. Also, **Atlas** was a collaborative project, and my commercial design work today involves a high degree of collaboration, although the ethos is entirely different from **Atlas**. I'm sure I'll find the need to collaborate again with others, but in a more open-ended way.

003z

X-RAY_8
JOHNNY BREWTON

FORMAT **135mm x 135mm**
MATERIAL **CARDBOARD BOX_SLIPCASE _RIBBON_ASSORTED LETTER PRESS CARDS_PHOTOGRAPHS_PAINTING**
TIME_PLACE **2001_USA**

www.xraybookco.com

Quote Johnny Brewton: The process itself is what motivates me to publish **X-Ray**. from digging through thrift shops and dumpsters looking for found materials, corresponding with collaborators and subscribers, designing, packaging, collating, assembling, folding, cutting, stitching, gluing, as well as the positive feedback reaction I get from those involved. In other words the process IS the project. I see it as raising these strange birds, teaching them to fly, hoping they go on and have good lives and are treated well.

X-ray no 8 – Out Now! postcard Edition limited to 126 copies. 100 numbered copies and 26 special lettered copies signed by contributors. Numbered copies available only at this time.

Contributors: Richard Brautigan, Giselle Brewton, Johnny Brewton, Charles Bukowski, Billy Childish, Jaime Crespo, Mike Daily, Brook Dalton, Jason Davis, Mart Faigenbaum, Dan Fante, Ed Galig, John Held Jr., Dave Holifield, Andy Jenkins, Gerald Locklin, Michael Montfort, Bern Porter, Herschel Silverman, Spo-Dee-O-Dee, Hunter S. Thompson, Chris Veitri, A. D. Winans, Mr. X

004z

CACTUS NETWORK_VOLITILE CIRCUS_8
CACTUS NETWORK

FORMAT **245mm x 350mm**
MATERIAL **SCREEN PRINTED CARDBOARD CASE_POSTER_STICKERS_MIXED MEDIA**
TIME_PLACE **1995_UK**

www.cactusnetwork.org.uk

Cactus developed out of the mail-art network, an off-shoot of the Situationist tradition of anonymous, subversive image making freed from the constraints of the gallery system. It was set up by a couple of designers interested in communicating ideas outside the confines of mainstream media, and with the intention of it being an international forum for debate, enabling colleagues in Eastern Europe to talk to their peers in the West by means of a few stamps. Initially contributors were asked to send in 150 copies of their artwork, which was then assembled by the pair of graphic designers, who insist on remaining anonymous, and returned to contributors without charge, as a boxed set. Though the designers weren't identified they left their mark on the packaging that changes with each issue. As the number of contributors increased they decided to turn the "collation" into a magazine; from issue 14 Cactus became a number of A4 pages given over to invited contributors, alongside mini-sized images from the general trawl. The stock, production methods and colour combinations were chosen by the designers.

005z

CACTUS NETWORK_CATAPULT_16
CACTUS NETWORK

FORMAT **210mm x 210mm**
MATERIAL **MIXED STOCK**
TIME_PLACE **1998_UK**

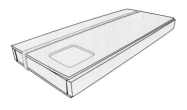

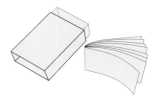

006z

DENNIS 33

FORMAT **110mm x 270mm**
MATERIAL **WOODEN BOX_MIXED MEDIA_ ELASTIC BAND_RIBBON_CONFECTIONERY**
TIME_PLACE **2001_THE NETHERLANDS**

007z

gunfight29_7
THE BOY LUCAS

EDITORS **LUCASANDCOE**
FORMAT **420mm x 145mm**
MATERIAL **HANDPAINTED COVER _MATT PAPER**
TIME_PLACE **2000_UK**

gunfight29@hotmail.com

008z

NASTY
STEPHEN BAKER

FORMAT **53mm x 77mm**
MATERIAL **MIXED STOCK_STRING**
TIME_PLACE **2000_AUSTRALIA**

hugh@sub.net.au

009z

FUEL_PRICE MATCHES?
FIRE FRIEND

FORMAT **38mm x 50mm**
MATERIAL **MATCHBOX_PHOTOCOPIES**
TIME_PLACE **2000_UK**

It's a cut-up box file and a whole lot more; including a gold-foil wrapped chocolate. The centre-fold slogan reads; Enlarge the rain forest, donate all office plants

Quote The Boy Lucas: gunfight29 was started by myself in January 2000, having just dropped out of art college and feeling fed up and uninspired by "art" as such. The magazine/print format was a perfect vehicle to combine all things I was interested in, e.g. words, photography, illustration, graphic design, music, culture, etc. and to be able to just do it and get it out to people; to make it available for public consumption. The immediacy of it was fantastic. Seven issues have so far been made, the last of which came out at the beginning of this year. It has been put on a bit of a back-burner due to other, more pressing commitments, such as the forthcoming album on Output, and also due to a lack of capital to invest in more ambitious print ideas. It has proved popular throughout the UK, selling well in Bristol and London. A highlight was selling copies in a shop dedicated to all things Bristol somewhere in Tokyo. John Coe joined me to co-produce gunfight29 from issue 6, and brought a strong design aesthetic to the mag. Avoiding advertising and all things corporate is very important to all involved, and is a big consideration affecting the future of gunfight29.

Producing gunfight29 has had big advantages, most of which have been getting to meet and talk with bands and people that have been an inspiration; such as, godspeedyoublackemperor!, Sigur Ros, Luke Vibert, the Pharcyde and Banksy.

A tiny zine collated from an old cut-up bible, over-painted in orange and interspersed with very un-Godly images of the band Kiss, and devilish quotes. All in all a blasphemous little number.

Housed in a customised matchbox (oh the symbolism), this tiny, photocopied gem is a purely visual anti-road-rage. Appropriating fragments of logos, biting statistics and an inky aesthetic, **Fuel, price matches?** is a thought provoking graphic bomb.

010z

NAME_IDENTITY
BEN CHONG, MATTHEW MCCARTHY,
TOBY MOORE, DAVID RECCHIA AND
ANDREW TREVILLIAN

FORMAT **220mm x 240mm**
MATERIAL **PAPER BAG_UNCOATED PAPER**
TIME_PLACE **1996_AUSTRALIA**

011z

NAME_OWNERSHIP_3
SIMON LEAH, MATTHEW MCCARTHY,
TOBY MOORE, DAVID RECCHIA AND
ANDREW TREVILLIAN

FORMAT **220mm x 200mm**
MATERIAL **UNCOATED PAPER**
TIME_PLACE **1997_AUSTRALIA**

012z

NAME_EVOLUTION
SIMON LEAH, MATTHEW MCCARTHY,
TOBY MOORE, DAVID RECCHIA AND
ANDREW TREVILLIAN

FORMAT **200mm x 200mm**
MATERIAL **UNCOATED PAPER**
TIME_PLACE **1999_AUSTRALIA**

013z

JOHNNY NO. 1
STEPHEN BAKER

FORMAT **95mm x 60mm**
MATERIAL **MIXED STOCK_SPIRAL BOUND**
TIME_PLACE **2000_AUSTRALIA**
PUBLISHER **HOUSE**

hugh@sub.net.au

An occasional, themed zine put together by a group of graphics students in Melbourne, Australia's city of design. After a call for entries went out to the art and design community a vast array of material was treated to various print techniques, paper stocks and graphic experimentation, within an economical, two-colour budget. Hand-tipped-in extras; stickers, found objects and individually painted covers complete a fascinating package. **Name** acted as a creative community builder throughout the late 90s.

Questionnaire
1. Is imitation flattery when it's your livelihood on the photocopier?
2. To what extent can you claim ownership over both the styles and trends you create and those you appropriate?
3. Can design ever truly be the property of the creator?

Metallic inks on card over appropriated mid-century imagry and cut-up, browning book pages. The whole chronicles the saga of Johnny in more or less legible text.

014z
DON'T PANIC
H. S. SOMMERVILLE

FORMAT **145mm x 210mm**
MATERIAL **BLUE ACETATE COVER_
CARTRIDGE PAPER**
TIME_PLACE **1996_UK**

015z
ON/OFF
H. S. SOMMERVILLE

FORMAT **135mm x 180mm**
MATERIAL **CARTRIDGE PAPER**
TIME_PLACE **1996_UK**

016z
KITTIES IN THE ENGINE
RANDY WOOD

FORMAT **70mm x 55mm**
MATERIAL **CARTRIDGE PAPER**
TIME_PLACE **1999_USA**

rwood@speakeasy.org

017z
WHAT YOU DON'T KNOW CAN HURT YOU
RYAN McGINNESS

FORMAT **2700mm x 130mm**
MATERIAL **CARTRIDGE PAPER**
TIME_PLACE **1994_USA**

ryan.mcginness@verzion.net

Quote Hugh Somerville: My self-published, hand-made story books are mainly concerned with myths, escapism, dreams and fear, and the positive and negative effects of each. Myths pervade all societies and cultures, ancient and modern, and effect our most intimate relationships. We use myths to reinvent ourselves and entertain others, but also to hide behind and dictate by. As with myths, we try to transcend reality through escapism and dreams as we're constantly redefining ourselves in dreams, which may lead to disappointment or free us to achieve fulfilment. Finally, fear produces conflicting tensions; it's what drives us forward and holds us back.

Another mini offering, this one frame per page comic is a cute, surreal (road) trip that causes a simultaneous reaction of, "ah" and "uh". From a prolific self-publishing, format busting, cartoonist.

Unrestricted by formats or disciplines, Ryan McGinness is as at home showing giant logos on enamel signs in a gallery as he is designing corporate identities and self-publishing zines, stickers and postcards. His work has appeared at New York's MOMA, Colette in Paris, and on the bottom of skateboards. Ryan's been quoted as saying; "A lot of art is boring".

018z
CHECK MY CHOPS_5
DAVE THE CHIMP

FORMAT **150mm x 480mm**
MATERIAL **CARTRIDGE PAPER**
TIME_PLACE **2000_UK**
PUBLISHER **MONKEY INDUSTRIES**

chimp@fold7.co.uk

019z
QUEEN OF THE UNIVERSE_5
JEANNETTE ORDAS

FORMAT **140mm x 215mm**
MATERIAL **CARTRIDGE PAPER**
TIME_PLACE **2000_CANADA**

nettiequeen@hotmail.com

020z
PLEASE SHUT UP MADAME
KAREN ELIOT, DON DAVENPORT,
SHAWNA VIRAGO AND ELVIS JOHNSON

FORMAT **105mm x 280mm**
MATERIAL **CARTRIDGE PAPER**
TIME_PLACE **1997_USA**

021z
PLOTZ_10_11_15
BARBARA KLIGMAN

FORMAT **140mm x 215mm**
MATERIAL **CARTRIDGE PAPER**
TIME_PLACE **1998-2001_USA**

plotz@pipeline.com

The Travel issue takes graf/graphic firebrand the Chimp to Japan, New York, Germany and California. Montaging his holiday snaps and Polaroids with cartooned observations of all sorts of visual stimulants, including facial hair, alongside hand-written diary extracts and silly speech-ballooned comments, this travelogue is a visual fest. Dave the Chimp is a regular self-publisher, on whatever subjects spring to mind.

This issue is dedicated to all the people who ever stepped on a skateboard and never stepped off.

Quote Jeannette Ordas: Doing my per-zine enables me to be creative and do something that is totally mine. I worked in record shops and offices and that certainly wasn't satisfying on any creative level. Plus, I love getting mail and free records!! It's all very selfish really.

Unless otherwise noted, all writings, curiosities, found art, layout, doodlings, editorial control, insecurities, spelling mistakes, typing and other menial tasks, are done by nettie, girl-wonder. Some girls will do anything for kicks.

A workplace zine for the call-centre Mc-jobbers, full of well written, humorous stuff and some inventive photocopy art, plus handy and effective, professional put downs.

"Just disconnect that fucker."
"I cannot understand you. I cannot understand you. I cannot understand you."
"Are you speaking English? I cannot tell."
"I have your home address and phone number. Do as I say, or I will cut your throat."
"Are you able to use a noun and a verb."
"Chew your food while I put you on hold, and then we'll talk."
"I won't be able to connect you."
"I AM the supervisor."
"Yes, I am a machine."
"No. Your call is NOT an emergency."
"My name is operator 666."
"Ah, so you are a solicitor."
"Bill collecting must be very rewarding work."
"You don't know your own phone number?"

Described by its editor as "a Jewish pop culture, humour-rant that sometimes gets out of hand". Barbara asks Jewish celebrities what they wore to their Bar Mitzvahs, translates yiddish and writes spoof media-genre copy, i.e. issues ape the TV Guide, Highlights (a mag aimed at good kids) and the Michelin Guide, all with a tongue-in-cheek, Jewish slant and wickedly doctored clip-art. She gained zine-world notoriety with an earlier title that prompted a "cease and desist" letter from the makers of a glamorous plastic doll.

Quote Barbara Kligman: My motivation comes from anger, disgust and basically not seeing or hearing a voice like mine out there in the mainstream or even in self-produced magazines. That's why I started the zine. I have something to say.

TV listing for the fachadded.
My name is Barbara and I am a TV-a-holic. The more my life (and this zine) change, the more I find myself retreating inside my tiny apartment with some tasty snacks and a nice program or two on the television. I love TV. I know it's not cool to say that but I do. Everything from "The Antiques Roadshow" to "Felicity" to freaky cable access shows (except for that guy on Sunday afternoons who plays his guitar to the radio. No. Wait. Even that), to old black and white movies to "The Naked Chef". And let's not even get me started about "Rhoda".
"The Antiques Roadshow" 8:00pm
WASPS in Their Natural Habitats
Big city appraisers go to the ding-dang civic centers in rural areas and small towns to over-estimate how much granpappy's broken musket can bring in gold pieces. Tonight: the nasty toy guy makes an old woman cry when he tells her that her beloved doll collection is a "hunka junk".

022z

ORIENTAL WHATEVER_7
DAN WU

ILLUSTRATION **LARK PIEN**
FORMAT **140mm x 215mm**
MATERIAL **CARTRIDGE PAPER**
TIME_PLACE **1999_USA**
PUBLISHER **YELLOW PERIL PRESS**

023z

JAPANIZE_1_2_3_4_8
TOKO

FORMAT **148mm x 210mm**
MATERIAL **CARTRIDGE PAPER**
TIME_PLACE **1999-2001_JAPAN**

toko.chan@virgin.net
tokojaco@hotmail.com

024z

THE CHAP_5_6_7_8_9_

EDITOR **GUSTAV TEMPLE**
DESIGN **VIC DARKWOOD**
FORMAT **148.5mm x 210mm**
MATERIAL **GLOSS COVER_MATT PAPER**
TIME_PLACE **2000_UK**

thechapmagazine.com

025z

CHICKEN HAWK
CLEON PETERSON AND
MISHA HOLLENBACH

FORMAT **140mm x 212mm**
MATERIAL **PHOTOCOPIES**
TIME_PLACE **1999_USA**

Quote Dan Wu: I've been making zines since high school (but not Oriental Whatever), so it's been a natural form of expression for me for a long time. My motivation was to make stuff I couldn't read elsewhere. Instead of waiting for someone else to come up with it, I just did it myself. As for Oriental Whatever, it was the same thing, there weren't many Asian American publications out there, so I thought I'd fill a void. On a personal level, I was just trying to create something that I'd want to read. To tell ya the truth, the zine is currently on hiatus. I'm working on my first short film, so that's taking up all my time and creative energy. I was on the edge of leaving zinedom (at least superficially, with the glossy cover and all) but opted to change direction, into film-making, instead of really tackling existential questions.

What's Hapa-ning? The Emergence of Hapa* Culture (*it's pronounced hopa) by Wei Ming Dariotis

What is culture? Is it shared language, religion, traditions, icons, food, art, music, dance, theater, fashion? Culture is often considered some amalgamation of all of these, but then what is the culture of hapas, people of mixed Asian heritage? We do not share a language – unless it is English, but that hardly defines us as a distinct cultural group. We do not share religion, traditions, food, etc. But we do often have certain shared experiences, such as being faced with the question, "What are you?" or knowing that we do not look, "racially", like either of our parents. And increasingly we do have shared icons, famous hapas, literature, art, theater, humor, even music and dance – as evidenced by the dance troupe, "In Mixed Company"...

Quote Toko: I like to see myself in my comic. I am looking for myself because I don't know who I am. I draw pennies (sic). but sometimes I feel so sad to draw man's pennies. Sometime I become very dirty woman. I draw blood in my comic; but sometimes I feel very sorry to draw blood. I have two faces in my comic and I enjoy to become the other person in my comic, so this is just my play world. I don't care if anybody criticises my comic; this is just my fan place. I am not sure of anything. Do I have to have a reason for everything? I think this is typical Japanese!!!

Fan letter

Dear Toko,
Being a poncey artist I regularly go to the ICA to buy intelligent and cutting edge magazines and fanzines. What I encountered on my last visit was your filthy piece of retrograde gutter trash. I haven't found anything so funny in ages...
Lee is my hero!

Thank you, Michael Smiles, London

Satirical gentleman's quarterly, The Chap, is fast achieving cult status. By taking a foppish (though decided un-PC) stance against Lad culture, it's tapped into a rich seam of readers who've moved on from the hectic pace of Loaded but aren't quite ready for the quiet life of Carp Monthly. It's currently being collated as a book and transformed into a TV show.

The author of the letter judged to be the best in the new issue of The Chap will receive the gentlemanly requisite featured in the current issue. This issue Captain Ian Gilmer receives a beautifully crafted pair of St. George elasticated arm bands.

SIR,
It appears I may have made a faux pas by propositioning the Ambassador's wife at a cocktail party at the British Embassy last week. She's a terribly pretty latino girl with mysterious dark eyes, a captivating smile, the shapeliest of legs and breasts that would make Wonderbras redundant. Unfortunately, I arrived slightly after the introductions had been made and, having been light of wallet for a considerable time, I'm afraid I made rather too much use of the free bar. One thing led to another and I apparently suggested to the lady, (in the local parlance), that we should "get naked, jump in the pool and do the wild thing". Although I could see she was tempted by my kind offer it appears she felt obliged to decline as, at the time I spoke, the band had stopped playing, the room was in virtual silence and the Ambassador was standing beside her. Once he had explained his matrimonial ties to the lady, I was compelled to make my excuses and leave, in fact, the Ambassador insisted on it and I now find my time in the tropics brusquely curtailed. I suppose it's a blessing in disguise that I can no longer afford ammunition for my old service revolver, as I may otherwise have had to "do the decent thing".
Captain Ian Gilmer (disgraced), Panama

Misha Hollenbach, aka, graf artist Perks, produces occasional themed zines working with various collaborators at home in Australia and abroad. He's been producing zines since childhood and uses his accumulated knowledge of print on promotional catalogues for PAM that mirror his zine-making sensibilities. PAM is a t-shirt label run with wife, Shauna aka Mini.

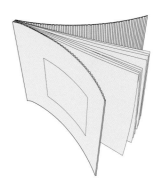

026z

YIN YANG
MISHA HOLLENBACH AND
SHAUNA TOOHEY

FORMAT **130mm x 175mm**
MATERIAL **UNCOATED PAPER**
TIME_PLACE **2000_AUSTRALIA**
PUBLISHER **PERKS AND MINI**

p_a_m@one.net.au

027z

WANKUSS
KEN OATH

FORMAT **105mm x 148mm**
MATERIAL **UNCOATED PAPER**
TIME_PLACE **2000_AUSTRALIA**

www.wankuss.com.au

A white trash, boys-own zine (with tongue firmly in cheek, I think), offering info on bong maintenance, urban myths, dragster racing, heavy metal t-shirt designs and plenty of toilet humour. Printed two-colour on heavy card, it'll stand up to some abuse.

Editorial, post winter 2000
Greetings from the loungeroom of Wankuss HQ.

I took on the job as Editor purely and simply because the ambitions of those in power at Wankuss are right up there with my own – namely to publish a magazine that will genuinely reflect and satisfy the needs of bogans nation-wide. Praise the lowered.

028z

ATTITUDE DANCER
REAS

FORMAT **210mm x 272mm**
MATERIAL **COATED COVER STOCK_
UNCOATED PAPER**
TIME_PLACE **2000_USA**

www.reasaok.com

Reas is an internationally acclaimed graf-inspired artist who works on paper, walls and canvas. This self-published Advanced Coloring Book shows sleazy, raunchy and tragic scenes of modern day American life, full of crowded beaches, super-fit bods, porno star attitude and guns.

029z

ARKITIP_1
SCOTT ANDREW SNYDER_AARON DEVINE
DEAN YOSHIHARA_MARK GONZALES_
MASON BROWN_EDWIN CARUNGAY

FORMAT **250mm x 255mm**
MATERIAL **CORRUGATED BOARD_
CARTRIDGE PAPER_STICKER_AUDIO REEL_
PLASTIC BAG**
TIME_PLACE **1999_USA**
PUBLISHER **ARKITIP**

www.arkitip.com

Quote Scott Andrew Snyder: I was working as an art director, freelance photographer and designer, but I was tired of creating and using my ideas for someone else's benefit. I have always been a magazine fanatic; collecting them, contributing to them and eventually wanting to create one of my own. Publishing Arkitip is a way for me to express myself while continuing to art direct artists that I respect and admire.

Arkitip enables people to enjoy original, unrestricted art, in a bimonthly periodical; the magazine is like a group show. Being an artist myself, I know that in doing commercial artwork, you always have hidden boundaries to adhere to.

With Arkitip, artists are allowed the freedom to just create, and that work is site specific to the magazine, thereby making it more collectable than just reproducing images that already exist. The fact that it's presented in a magazine, and at a lower price than what hangs on a gallery wall, makes it available to art collectors of all economic levels. Each issue edition is a different size and shape, it's hand-stamped and numbered in limited quantities and is itself like an original piece of art.

030z

ARKITIP_4
SCOTT ANDREW SNYDER_TOBIN YELLAND
HARMONY KORINE_MISHA HOLLENBACH
AND GREEN LADY

FORMAT **210mm x 140mm**
MATERIAL **SCREEN PRINT COVER**
_CARTRIDGE PAPER_STAPLES
TIME_PLACE **2000_USA**
PUBLISHER **ARKITIP**

031z

ARKITIP_9_SPACE TRAVEL
SCOTT ANDREW SNYDER_
DALEK_ROSTARR_MICHAEL LEON
AND JOSEPH KRAL

FORMAT **250mm x 250mm**
MATERIAL **PERFECT BOUND_**
SHRINKWRAPPED_PATCHES
TIME_PLACE **2001_USA**
PUBLISHER **ARKITIP**

032z

APPEARANCES ARE OFTEN DECEPTIVE
HIRO SUGIYAMA AND
TOMOYUKI YONEZU

FORMAT **140mm x 180mm**
MATERIAL **GLOSS BOARD**
TIME_PLACE **1997_JAPAN**
PUBLISHER **ENLIGHTENMENT**

hougado@netjoy.ne.jp

A perfectly detailed appropriation of a
child's picture book, complete with thick
card, high gloss leaves and "safety"
rounded corners. The white cover gives
nothing away, heightening the shock of
familiar cuddly icons, subtly altered to the
point of grotesque mutilation. These
surreal re-takes on cute are cleanly
presented, minus the gore, in sickeningly
rich full-colour.

033z

ZONDER TINTEL
MAMA_BORIS VAN BERKUM_
MARK VAN BEEST_MAYA VAN EERDEN
MARTIJN VAN BERTRAM

FORMAT **150mm x 150mm**
MATERIAL **STICKERS_ELASTIC BAND**
TIME_PLACE **1998_THE NETHERLANDS**

www.mama.ipr.nl

A totally unique publication about street-
inspired artist Johan Boer who guerrilla-
pastes work onto the windows of elitist art
galleries. Printed as stickers, with the gloss
side showing the artist at work and the
matte-backing carrying info, the various
sized sheets are folder four times to create
leaves of two different widths. The whole is
temporarily bound with red elastic, so
users may unravel the pages and stick
them wherever.

034z

WORLD OF PAIN
JAMES JARVIS

FORMAT **165mm x 258mm**
MATERIAL **COATED PAPER**
TIME_PLACE **2001_UK**
PUBLISHER **SILAS AND MARIA**

035z

FRESH UPS_1
PINKY

FORMAT **170mm x 258mm**
MATERIAL **CARTRIDGE PAPER**
TIME_PLACE **1998_UK**
PUBLISHER **PINKY D. R. A.**

036z

MYCOSE_7_10_11
BOSLEY_GOF_GENTIANE_P'TIT MARC_
B. MONTI_JÉROME

FORMAT **140mm x 190mm**
MATERIAL **SCREENPRINTED COVER_
COLOURED PAPER_POSTER**
TIME_PLACE **2000-2001_BELGIUM**

bosley66@hotmail.com
genti@netcourrier.com

037z

DRAWINGS
RON TURNER

FORMAT **295mm x 280mm**
MATERIAL **PHOTOCOPY PAPER_
COLOURED CARD COVER_METAL SCREWS**
TIME_PLACE **1998_CANADA**

Quote James Jarvis: **World of Pain** is a comic I produced. It's just a catchy title and a vehicle for all my concerns about consumerism and that kind of thing. I was asked to do an exhibition in Japan and instead of compiling a retrospective, I wanted to do something that was more about me, so I made the comic. It took about a month and it's quite limited because I'm so obsessive and worried about making something perfect. For me, the most pure way to express a thought is to make a drawing. It's the most efficient, dynamic and quick process. The content of what I do has always been important too. My characters are actors, and in **World of Pain** they're feeling despair at the pain of existence! But they're also innocent, just by the fact that they're cartoon characters means they have an innocence to them. Every time they see something bad it brings them down, then the next minute they're happy again.

Quote Pinky: God bless the photocopier!

The world famous catalogue of novelties, gags, optical illusions, magic tricks and weird shit!

Warning: Always share your **Fresh Ups** with friends, neighbours and relatives.

Published by Pinky D. R. A., a hand drawn division of the Devious Rebels Corporation, est. 1986.

Similarities between any characters in this publication and any living or dead is just in your twisted little mind!!

A comix zine, with various stock and cover treatments, which presents a wide range of graphic styles and content, some dark phycosis to jolly, blobby characters.

A self-publisher and prolific drawer, Ron's sketches of everyday life and found artwork are in a refreshingly direct graphic style. The larger, folio-style book is held together with substantial metal screws while the other smaller, tape-bound format, offers up an intense series of drawings dating from July 28 to November 25, 1992.

038z

DRAWINGS
RON TURNER

FORMAT **145mm x 180mm**
MATERIAL **PHOTOCOPY PAPER**
TIME_PLACE **1992_CANADA**
PUBLISHER **MANIFESTO PRESS**

039z

MO'GUMBO
ROSS PRIDDLE

FORMAT **215mm x 280mm**
MATERIAL **CARTRIDGE PAPER**
TIME_PLACE **2000_CANADA**
PUBLISHER **IMP PRESS**

An exercise in degradation; a page of type is repeatedly photocopied until it assumes a form more organic than informational.

040z

FOUND
RYDER P. MOSES

FORMAT **140mm x 215mm**
MATERIAL **CARTRIDGE PAPER**
TIME_PLACE **1998_USA**

ryderpmoses@hotmail.com

Quote Ryder P. Moses, aka, Presley: It seems to me that our cities are awash in images that can be readily plucked from the streets. I find many of these to be very beautiful and natural, no different than a flower or a majestic landscape. By collecting and photocopying these "found" images I can easily and cheaply share them with friends.

041z

SHOREDITCH TWAT_2_3_5_6_10_11_12
NEIL BOORMAN

DESIGN **BUMP**
FORMAT **148mm x 210mm**
MATERIAL **CARTRIDGE PAPER**
TIME_PLACE **2000_UK**
PUBLISHER **3RD FLOOR**

Shoreditch Twat is an abrasive critique of the "fashionable" London club and bar scene in and around that particular east of the City neighbourhood. Deliberately lo-fi, its raw visuals (by design team Bump) and acerbic comedy (with anonymous contributions from a host of in-the-know media stars) have gained it notoriety and a devoted following. It's free and it's everywhere.

DJ Bird #11
DJ Bird is the infamous porn-fi DJ's moll who chronicled her exploits in the magazine **Sleaze Nation**, 1997-1998. **Shoreditch Twat** has rather unfortunately acquired this previously unpublished DJ Bird article on the ins and outs of record shops.

Records! Life is too short to play silly games. Pick a thing – anything, and take the fucking living piss out of it. Cut corners, overtake on the inside and sleep with stupid DJs. You have everything to loose but nothing. Nothing. No one will hate you for it (they already hated you before), they'll just remember you. Take records and their shops for example. Take them seriously and you'll be lost, utterly lost. Take the piss and you'll be made up. Record shops are run by pricks for pricks. So best just sit on them and watch the free vinyl flood into your free lap dance. Weird emporiums filled with Carhartted vinyl-obsessed men. Weird, weird boys with self-conscious hair and play-lists badly tattooed into their shallow insecure hearts. Records!...

042z

BLOW_1_5
JAMES PRETLOVE AND
MICHAEL OLIVEIRA-SALAC

FORMAT **210mm x 297mm**
MATERIAL **PHOTOCOPIES_RIVETTED SPINE**
TIME_PLACE **1993_UK**

043z

MYSTERY DATE_1_2_3_4_5_6
LYNN PERIL

FORMAT **140mm x 215mm**
MATERIAL **CARTRIDGE PAPER**
TIME_PLACE **1994-1999_USA**

www.pinkthink.com

044z

SWEET SHOP
ANTHONY BURRILL

FORMAT **210mm x 297mm**
MATERIAL **COATED PAPER**
TIME_PLACE **1998_UK**

www.anthonyburrill.com
anthony@friendchip.com

045z

AMP_8_10
ANNE-MARIE PAYNE

DESIGN **LOOK AT ME**
FORMAT **148mm x 210mm**
MATERIAL **CARTRIDGE PAPER**
TIME_PLACE **1998-2001_UK**

www.ampnet.co.uk

A piss-taking, guerrilla fashion magazine that began life as a ream of grainy photocopies, before transforming into a lavishly designed, perfect bound, die-cut tome. Also, resting not dead.

Quote Michael Blow: We did **Blow** because we wanted to do something that was defining and documenting the 90s. When we started **Blow**, 80s attitudes were still very present, and there was so much happening that was not being covered by the mainstream press at the time. We wanted to change all that and prove that a magazine could be successful without all the usual massive financial investment and bolloxs meetings and plans etc. **Blow** was also a showcase for work from extremely talented people who've gone off to do pretty well.

Cold Calling #1

Blow Magazine telephoned everybody on page 270 of the London L-Z directory and asked the burning fashion question of the moment – "You've been given £115 to buy a pair of Gucci clogs, what would you spend the money on?" – and found that not all of London is queuing for clogs.

"Do you know, you people really piss me off. Where did you get my number? (page 270 of the London telephone directory) Well we don't want to buy shoes or anything so go away..."

"Oh I don't know. I have to wear certain shoes – those would be too modern for me I'm sure."

"I don't even know what they are. What did you say? Goo Clogs?"

"Are you being serious? I'd probably go to the Armani sale and buy something there."...

Quote Lynn Peril: What motivates me? Well, my zine is an excellent outlet for my obsession with vintage prescriptive material; home economics texts, charm and beauty guides, sex education and dating manuals, and etiquette books. It gives me a chance to share what I've learned and a good reason to buy more books! Doing a zine actively alleviates boredom in a way the passive watching of television never can. Because of the zine, my mailbox is rarely empty, and I've made friends all over the world. Zine-making is anti-corporate by nature. And, of course, it's fun!"

A Word from the Editrix #6

Menstrual Update

It was bound to happen. While researching the last issue, I literally spent hours at the library going through Walt Disney (oh, wait, I am allowed to use that term without paying royalties?) filmographies, biographies, even websites looking for the release date of "The Story of Menstruation". But my search was in vain. It was almost as if the Disney Corporation had purged all mention of "The Story of Menstruation" from its files. Then in the space of three days in November, I found not one but two mentions of the film! The first came from a 1957 issue of **The Journal of Home Economics** (oh, baby, oh, baby, oh, oh, oh!)...

Quote Anthony Burrill: I've always been a fan of small-scale, self-published ephemera and I started collecting Jake Tilson's **Atlas**. Then I produced my own books, postcards, etc. at college. After I left, when budgets were non existent, I began making photocopied books to send to people, as sort of mini-portfolios. These books became an end in themselves with each having its own theme. I even had a stall at the Small Press Fair once and sold a few copies! I think my main motivation for making the books was to spread my work around and to have a "product" that people could identify with me. (Basically, I just like making them and sending them to friends).

Quote Anne-Marie Payne: I wanted to be a writer and had no idea how to go about becoming one. My inspirations, Erica Smith of **GirlFrenzy** and Lucy Sweet of **Unskinny**, were no longer publishing, and I was desperate to read more of the same kind of stuff – stuff produced by and for young people without the mediation of an editor in thrall to the marketing department, so I started **Amp**. I also like the perversity of producing a free magazine in a capitalist culture; and I make cool friends.

#10
A recent review of **Amp** described it as "the zine which revels in females – lusty; fleshy; sweat and blood and all". And it does. **Amp** loves the ladies. Girls are clever, interesting, intricate, full of details; glittery green lines painted on their eyelids, shimmery things round their necks, and always, somewhere, a purse full of secrets – tubes of glitter, brushes with dark dust on their tips, bottles of foundation which come undone and paint their handbags skintone.

Bra-clad beauties, corset cuties: the best bra shop ever. Suki Kent

Halfway down Rye Lane in Peckham, just across from Netto, is a shrine to womanhood. The window is stuffed with mannequins in cantilevered bras and tight, tight girdles, while long plastic legs sport unusual stockings: fine fishnets with glittery seams running down the back, nylons with diamante bows at the ankles, pink knee-highs. Inside are racks of big lace panties, babydoll nighties, and every kind of bra imaginable. The tiny changing-room has a sloping ceiling, a blue curtain, and a little table with a radio, a box of tissues and a deodorant. The atmosphere is intimate, secretive, sensual, and faintly embarrassing; think flirty Fifties, not nasty Nineties. Think Beauty Parade and Betty Page, not **Loaded**. Regan Corsetier belongs to a saucier era, when a glimpsed bra-strap could drive a man to drink, and ruin a girl's reputation in an instant. Our kinda place!

046z

CHEAP DATE_4
KIRA JOLLIFFE

COVER **FERGADELIC FOR HYSTERIC GLAM**
FORMAT **210mm x 297mm**
MATERIAL **CARTRIDGE PAPER_SPRAY PAINT**
TIME_PLACE **1998_UK**

047z

PATTI_DESTINY ISSUE
J. T. ANZAI, JESSE BIRCH,
ASHLEY CHADWICK, DYLAN DOUBT,
LESLIE GRANT, WARREN HILL, JANE LEE,
KIM MONROE, ALEX TERZICH

FORMAT **200mm x 130mm**
MATERIAL **COATED PAPER**
TIME_PLACE **2000_CANADA**
PUBLISHER **PATTI MEDIA EMPIRE**

patti_magazine@hotmail.com

048z

CRUST
RICK PINCHERA

FORMAT **212mm x 140mm**
MATERIAL **SCREEN PRINT**
COVER_CARTRIDGE PAPER
TIME_PLACE **USA**
PUBLISHER **TOP SHELF PRODUCTIONS**

www.topshelfcomix.com

049z

STREET RAT BAG_3
RATical AND RITA RODENTIA

ILLUSTRATION **RITA RODENTIA**
FORMAT **215mm x 280mm**
MATERIAL **GLOSS COVER_
CARTRIDGE PAPER**
TIME_PLACE **2001_CANADA**

Welcome! to the ever-changing world of the thinking thrifter! But before I say anything else I must tell you to check out the free flexidisc of a Cigarettes song! – a very exciting and rare thing that we've somehow managed to get together for you (and of course we assume you still have a vinyl record player). Apart from that, as you can see we interviewed the unspeakably cool Joan Jett, inventor-with-a-heart Clive Sinclair and anti-fashion person Wayne Hemingway. And that's not all, well look for yourselves!

Quote Leslie Grant: There are quite a few reasons that we all had for starting Patti. We share the desire to produce an alternative to current fashion and art magazines because we saw a lack of critical yet humourous approaches in print. We want to make sure Patti is a critique, but without being completely separate from either fashion or art magazines so that it can potentially participate in a dialogue with each genre (we try to avoid being pigeon-holed into the "zine" category). We also want to make sure that Patti is not merely a negative text, but that it showcases new talent and ideas, with a forward-looking perspective; and we think that the print media is the ideal way to get ideas out to the largest audience. In the future we would like Patti to be less expensive, and widely distributed, in keeping with the idea that art can be disseminated on a grand scale and does not reside strictly in galleries and museums, both of which are loaded, controlled space. Fashion is another highbrow phenomenon that Patti hopes to recontextualise for the average reader; in a do-it-yourself manner, and also by supporting emerging designers. Patti strives to make the presentation of culture more accessible to all practitioners, and we're always eager for submissions and new blood.

Rick Pinchera lives in Jamaica Plain, Massachusetts with his lovely wife and produces a regular cartoon strip for the Willamette Week, in Portland, OR. Here it's been collated by local small publisher, Top Shelf Productions, into zine form. The logo appropriates a well-known, household product, while the banal daily exploits of the edgy Gen-X characters will be just as familiar to young urbanites the world over.

Front Cover: "I reckon it's time..." sign, etta cetera: Street Rat-Bag logos, Babynous: "Place" stamps, H. R. Fricker: fotos of Lachlan Simpson and painted wall, etta cetera: layout, RATical and Rita Rodentia.

Money Schmoney – Alternative Currencies
Rita Rodentia
Hey! Did you know that there are hundreds of communities out there that use alternative currencies? That is money systems that are created by the community, for the community and actually help to loosen the grip that multi-national corporations have on the throats of our towns and cities. First of all, I think one of the main strategies we should be implementing in our fight against the self-proclaimed government is creating alternatives to every single institution they provide. (I'm talking schools, health-care, food, work, homes – all that stuff). Not that it needs to be done on a large scale – start with you and your neighbors. That's the way the Global Exchange Network started in Argentina...

050z

TEMP SLAVE_9
KEFFO

ILLUSTRATION **PETER SICKMAN-GARNER**
FORMAT **175mm x 215mm**
MATERIAL **CARTRIDGE PAPER**
TIME_PLACE **1999_USA**

051z

HOLIDAY IN THE SUN_NEW YORK
JIM MUNROE

B/W ILLUSTRATION **PATRICIO DAVILA**
FORMAT **140mm x 207mm**
MATERIAL **CARTRIDGE PAPER**
TIME_PLACE **1999_CANADA**
PUBLISHER **LICK SPITTLE VENTURES**

jim@yip.org

052z

KACHINA_23
MONA WEINER

FORMAT **140mm x 215mm**
MATERIAL **CARTRIDGE PAPER**
TIME_PLACE **2000_USA**

053z

NONONZENZ
anand zenz

FORMAT **145mm x 207mm**
MATERIAL **CARTRIDGE PAPER**
TIME_PLACE **2000_UK**

zenz@theculture.net

Pissing on the work ethic. This essay originally appeared in the political journal **Out of Bounds**. I liked it so much that I'm reprinting it here in the pages of **Temp Slave**! Written by Tom Wheeler, the essay pretty much says it all in regards to work.

I despise work. It's not that I'm lazy or that I hate the idea of working. There are plenty of good things worth working for. What I dislike is the institution of work. In these days of falling living standards, lower expectations, dead end jobs and temp work, the workplace is increasingly becoming a hostile place. I should know. It doesn't take much to lose your job these days. I've been fired from two jobs in just the past five months. The last job really sucked the shit out of my septic tank. It was quite a relief to get fired from that one. I can also thank my parasitic, tyrannical bosses for instilling in me a contemptible aversion to employment. In today's economy there are thousands, perhaps millions of people each year desperately searching for employment yet are unable to find any. My question is, why bother? You see I've come to the conclusion that it isn't money that is the root of all evil. I believe that "work" as it is currently defined, is the root of all evil. Work is forced labor. Work sucks. For anyone who values freedom and liberty, the workplace should be recognized as the one place where democracy does not exist...

Quote Jim Munroe: I was reading Stephen Duncombe's **Zines, notes from the underground** and was inspired by the serious (but not pedantic) tone that he gave to the whole discussion on the politics of underground/mainstream cultural tension. I wanted to add my own little bit to this – and I also felt it was my responsibility to tell my story as explicitly as possible, so that zinesters and writers in general could get an insider's perspective on the book industry.

The book deal looms large in our cultural imagination. For writers, it's a ticket to a place they've heard about all their lives – a destination where the buffets are free, it never rains, and there's all the time in the world to chit-chat by the pool. A holiday in the sun. When they get there, some find there's few vegetarian options. They long for rain to echo their mood on sad days. And the people who lounge by the pool are silent, wondering how much the others paid for the trip. I've been on holiday for a year now and I'm not what you'd call silent. My opinion is that the whole thing is overrated. I published zines and books myself for eight years before I signed with HarperCollins – so unlike many writers, this wasn't my first trip away from home and I wasn't as giddily excited. A lot of people will consider me ungrateful, but that presupposes that a publisher is doing a writer a favor – a power imbalance that impacts our culture considerably. In the interest of draining some of the guild-like power of the publishing world and putting it in the hands of artists, I've decided on full disclosure. There's a weird complicity of silence between publishers and authors not to discuss what goes on, mostly because both the houses and the authors stand to gain stature from the public assuming million-dollar advances. So from the dollar figures to the emotional repercussions, this zine is my effort to arm writers with some realistic expectations. Consider it a straight-talkin' travel guidebook as compared with the glossy brochure.

Okay, so I know the format of this zine changes every time I do it, but you have to forgive me. It's going to be this size from now on, because it's the cheapest (at five cents a page) and easiest. No cutting, just folding. So I'm sorry if it's kind of boring or whatnot but I really can't do anything about it. I'm a poor college student who is forced to spend all of her time doing academic nonsense instead of fun stuff like writing zines.

How many white boys are going to complain about how much the world has screwed them over before people get sick of it? Limp Bizkit, Korn, Eminem...

Since 1988, anand zenz has produced statements on t-shirts. This is the second edition of the catalogue of statements which are currently available. The order of the statements is also a rough chronology of their origination. Some statements from the previous catalogue have been replaced or altered (denoted by:*). All statements after statement fifty are also new to this edition. This print run: May 2000, copies 1750 to 4750.

054z

CLAREMONT ROAD_THE END OF THE BEGINNING
CLARE ZINE

FORMAT **150mm x 210mm**
MATERIAL **CARTRIDGE PAPER**
TIME_PLACE **1994_UK**

055z

THE SPRINT_LIBERATING THE ANGEL_7

FORMAT **210mm x 297mm**
MATERIAL **PHOTOCOPIES**
TIME_PLACE **1996_UK**

056z

COME ON IN! THE WAR'S FINE
TOBY TRIPP

FORMAT **105mm x 148mm**
MATERIAL **COLOURED COVER_
CARTRIDGE PAPER_PLASTIC BAG**
TIME_PLACE **2001_UK**
PUBLISHER **WELCOME PUBLISHING**

tobytripp@feelwelcome.co.uk

057z

TWO STEAKS_6
STEPHEN STEWART

FORMAT **148mm x 210mm**
MATERIAL **CARTRIDGE PAPER**
TIME_PLACE **2000_UK**

twosteaks@hotmail.com

One by one we were led out of the street for the last time as we knew it – dirty and tired, we were asked time and time again how we felt at the end of Claremont Road. Time and time again came the reply, "This isn't the end, mate, this is just the beginning!"

On the first day of December 1994, our colourful community was evicted and our vibrant street bulldozed in the wake of the M11 Link Road. The eviction lasted four and a half days, the longest in post war history, and cost the government millions, but the experience of the street and the struggle it became will never be forgotten.

Claremont Road, the end of the beginning
is a collection of writings, artworks, poems, songs, images and ideas, intended as a creative tribute to a very creative place, with contributions from some of the thousands that visited or lived on the street.

Thanx to all contributors and the Department of Transport and Michael Howard for bringing us all together. Enjoy!
Clare Zine

This account of Street Party #2 is one section of a text about the environmental impacts of the spectacular commodity economy, in particular the motor car industry.

Four other sections appeared in previous issues of **The Sprint** in the 1980s and were based on chapters of a manuscript I first wrote for Penguin Education in the early 1970s, originally intended for publication by them. At the time the editor rejected the text on the grounds that it was "snobbishly anti-car" (and anti-capitalist). I then dropped the project after declining to work with a "ghost" writer. Penguin Education was closed down by its holding company, Penguin Books and since then my former editor has become an environmentalist. I decided to "go public" again and produce a text in serialised, low budget format after going to some recent street and cycling demonstrations and to the Newbury camps.

Cartoonist Toby Tripp publishes mini-chapbooks of his droll strips. Regular characters include a family of lively skeletons, a host of animated house-hold objects and a couple of "hoodie"-clad neo-lads who, in this issue, find themselves conscripted to play war.

Two Steaks is a classic fanzine dedicated to the band Idlewild. With the simplest of means, A4 photocopies and a staple per issue, Stephen creates an intimate, but visually spacious, insider's guide for fans.

Quote Stephen Stewart: I like messing around with words and images and having people I respect appreciate it. The fanzine is a forum for my ideas.

058z

VERTIGO_6

ILLUSTRATION **ERICA SMITH**
FORMAT **175mm x 175mm**
MATERIAL **CARTRIDGE PAPER**
TIME_PLACE **1997_UK**

059z

UNTALENTED FOOLS
MOLLY M. CANNON AND TARA J. McCAW

FORMAT **140mm x 215mm**
MATERIAL **COLOURED PAPER**
TIME_PLACE **1996_2001_USA**

http://untalentedfool.tripod.com
untalentedfools@yahoo.com

060z

PINK MOON_A NICK DRAKE FANZINE_3
JASON CREED

FORMAT **148mm x 210mm**
MATERIAL **CARTRIDGE PAPER**
TIME_PLACE **1995_2001_UK**

www.nickdrakeworld.com

061z

MONK MINK PINK PUNK_6
JOSH RONSEN

FORMAT **140mm x 220mm**
MATERIAL **TIN FOIL_MIXED MEDIA**
TIME_PLACE **1999_USA**

jronsen@my-deja.com
http://www.flash.net/~jronsen/mmpp/in
dex.html.

An essential guide to groovy living in the sea-side town of Brighton, complete with pub guides, how to survive a gig, best surf spots world-wide and zine reviews.

A pop art guide to pirate radio, written and illustrated by the south-coast pop art experimentalists.

You will need the following; a tape, some energy and an idea!

Prepare a taped programme using a small tape recorder, using the pause control to perform minor edits. Once completed, the recorder can be connected to a transmitter and the show played back over the air. Improve your set-up as you need to; a cheap microphone can turn your stereo system into a low-cost recording studio. You could even use a mixer and do decks, tapes and voices all at once!

Transmitter – buy a used one from your local classified columns or amateur radio store. Check the internet for more technical shit; search for "radio resistors". Frequency – monitor one for several days to check it's clear. Try around 41 meters to start with – it has the least interference and the most listeners. You could even operate your station on the move. Drive around the hills near your town or leave your gear transmitting overnight from way on up high! Knowledge is the best weapon. Know your gear, use it properly, with common sense and trustworthy pals.

Utterly hilarious and totally amateur, in an uninhibited scrawlly way, and, highly readable for it.

Quote Molly Cannon and Tara McCaw: This brain-child was spawned in the summer of 1996 as an outlet for our satiric commentary on the popular culture that was smothering our teenage creativity. From the Spice Girls to Hootie to "What if God was one of us?" we were suffocating in a sea of oppressive images...yadda yadda yadda. Of course, we're lying. We just wanted to write about jams. We had a hard time choosing a medium conducive to expressing our unequivocal support for that long-lost fashion genius of the 1980s; long, colourful shorts. Fortunately, we stumbled on the zine and quickly realised the marketing potential for our on the side rock band, the Untalented Fools. While the zine wasn't really needed, since the music speaks for itself, the issues just seemed to spontaneously generate. Besides, there's not much else to do in Wheaton, MD, when you're 15. Tara (ukelele) will be 21 next week, and Molly (kazoo) will be 21 in October, but we still live in Wheaton. The rest is history.

#Free Advice
1. Pen chewing can be just as effective as expensive therapy sessions.
2. Energy vampires lurk in malls.
3. The TV Guide is sometimes wrong.
4. The key to cool – teen people magazines.
5. Some people are real mean.
6. Don't ignore cork damage.
7. All the super heroes live in the city.
8. The "Big C" is coming watch your back.
9. Don't worship monkeys.
10. In a pinch prostitution is just as good as an ATM.

Quote Jason Creed: Paul Weller mentioned Nick Drake in an interview, so I bought an album, and lying in my room listening to it, I thought, I need to know about this guy. Where normally you'd just pick up a magazine, there was nothing. So I started buying old issues of the NME and reading reviews and asking people for information, and I got enough stuff together for three issues, so I put them out simultaneously. I thought that's that, I'll probably sell ten copies (it became the best selling fanzine in London's specialist music store, Helter Skelter). The response was overwhelming. People sent more info and I ended up doing 19 issues. But the more I dug, and the more you know about someone, you realise that you don't really know them at all. Now the information is on a website, I've lost interest in the little printed things and have no interest in knowing more. Nick Drake's albums have been re-mastered and re-issued and more material is still being found. But, for me, the zine is dead.

In writing Pink Moon, I have simply tried to put down facts about Nick's life, without including any conjecture. But, considering I was only two years old when Nick died, it's hard to know if everything you read about him is totally accurate. So if anyone knows anything contrary to what I have written, then please let me know and I will set the record straight in a future issue.

Quote Josh Ronsen: MMPP has been very, very neglected lately. I started it because I wanted to write for a zine, and a zine editor said that I should submit something to be considered, but I just decided to make my own and then I wouldn't have to worry about trying to convince someone that a ten-page interview with so and so was worth publishing. #7 is published on-line.

I've been very busy since then, doing what, I can't say, but it's taken all of my time...I have a mail art project going on right now where I send people 39 words culled from a Lawrence Durrell novel and ask them to write a new short text using those 39 words (in order!). I have about a dozen responses so far, and some of them are amazing! This will be published as an MMPP issue sometime soon.

062z

LOUD PAPER_V2.3_V3.2
MIMI ZEIGER AND JEREMY XAVIER

COVER **CYNTHIA CONNOLLY AND JASON GRIFFITHS**
FORMAT **137mm x 212mm**
MATERIAL **CARTRIDGE PAPER**
TIME_PLACE **1998_USA**

loudpaper@excite.com

063z

LOUD PAPER_V3.4
MIMI ZEIGER

ILLUSTRATION **JED MORFIT**
DESIGN **TAYLER KIM AND ENRIQUE MOSQUEDA**
FORMAT **212mm x 280mm**
MATERIAL **CARTRIDGE PAPER**
TIME_PLACE **2000_USA**

064z

HEAD_AMBIENT FISHY ISSUE_6
MOBILE D UNIT AND FACELESS NETWORKER

FORMAT **278mm x 206mm**
MATERIAL **COATED PAPER_STICKER**
TIME_PLACE **1996_UK**

head@headmedia.demon.co.uk

065z

THE GRUESOME ACTS OF CAPITALISM
PUBLIC RECORD

FORMAT **140mm x 215mm**
MATERIAL **COLOURED PAPER**
TIME_PLACE **1998_CANADA**
PUBLISHER **GET TO THE POINT**

meccanormal@msm.com
http://meccanormal.tripod.com
meccanormal@hotmail.com

Loud paper is dedicated to increasing the volume of architectural discourse. It is a slambamgetitoutthere way of linking architectural thoughts, musings and new work with the culture at large. **Loud paper** is open to all students, architects, educators, girls about town, dear Johns and critics as a place for writing loud about architecture and culture. Submissions of articles, projects, book and music reviews are encouraged.

v3.4
Six (Interrupted) Views of the Sky
Artist's statement: As far as I can tell, magazines are like Tokyo real estate; space is at a premium. Afforded the luxury of a six-page spread, my immediate reaction was to create a series of images that would take full advantage of the luxury, as well as provide a counter-point to the usual visual density of the magazine page. My thought was that by using a few, simplified black images in the foreground, I would draw the readers' focus to the background, and to the relatively rare, serenity of the blank page.

Jed Morfit is an artist and illustrator in San Francisco. He can be reached at fmera@hotmail.com.

Intro
After a time of decay comes the turning point. The powerful light that has been banished returns. There is movement, but it is not brought about by force....The movement is natural, arising spontaneously. For this reason the transformation of the old becomes easy. The old is discarded and the new is introduced. Both measures accord with the time; therefore no harm results...Information should be free, without any form of artificial restraint or control, such as is upheld by the legal system and copyright. Plagiarise, remix, cut up, fuck up...this is the basis for all creativity and progress. A desire to remain outside of the media game show is necessary if one wishes to retain independence of thought and action. Anonymity is subversive. While living / Be a dead man / Be completely dead / And then do as you please / And all will be well.

"We're not dropping out, we're infiltrating, and taking over."

Listen to the @mbience...

Quote David Lester: On an intellectual level I'm surrounded by the cultural assaults of mainstream prattle; the dwindling down of ideas for mass appeal; the death of ideals and the lack of romance for a better world. It is unfashionable to feel, to do anything except for a profit motive.

There is still great popular work produced in spite of themarketplace. I know that and I don't dismiss everything. But it seems the world's window is open only so much, includes only so much. This tiny window does not allow for much diversity. The larger our communication portals are, the smaller our words become. So in this context I look at zines, chapbooks etc. as an important political/cultural response. Our societies need an "underground". On another level, ever since I was a kid, I spent my time drawing and making little books. Who knows what I was thinking or where I got these ideas from. Kind of frightening to think I'm still doing the same things now, or maybe that's okay. But I've always loved books, comix, magazines, newspapers. The publication of ideas is endless. Self-publication becomes an act of defiance, hence the imprint, Smarten UP! & Get To The Point, run by me and Jean Smith (my partner in Mecca Normal). My other publishing projects have just kind of developed by happy chance. Of course it's a lot of work and I fit things in where I can. I've got a full length book of drawings looking for a publisher; my band Mecca Normal is playing a festival next month in Olympia, WA, and an autumn tour with Unwound in the eastern USA; and I design a quarterly newspaper on books. I treat my apartment as a creative laboratory (drawing table, amp, guitar, paints, brushes, pens and paper etc). Everyday it is exciting to get up and feel in one's hands the heat of the first coffee.

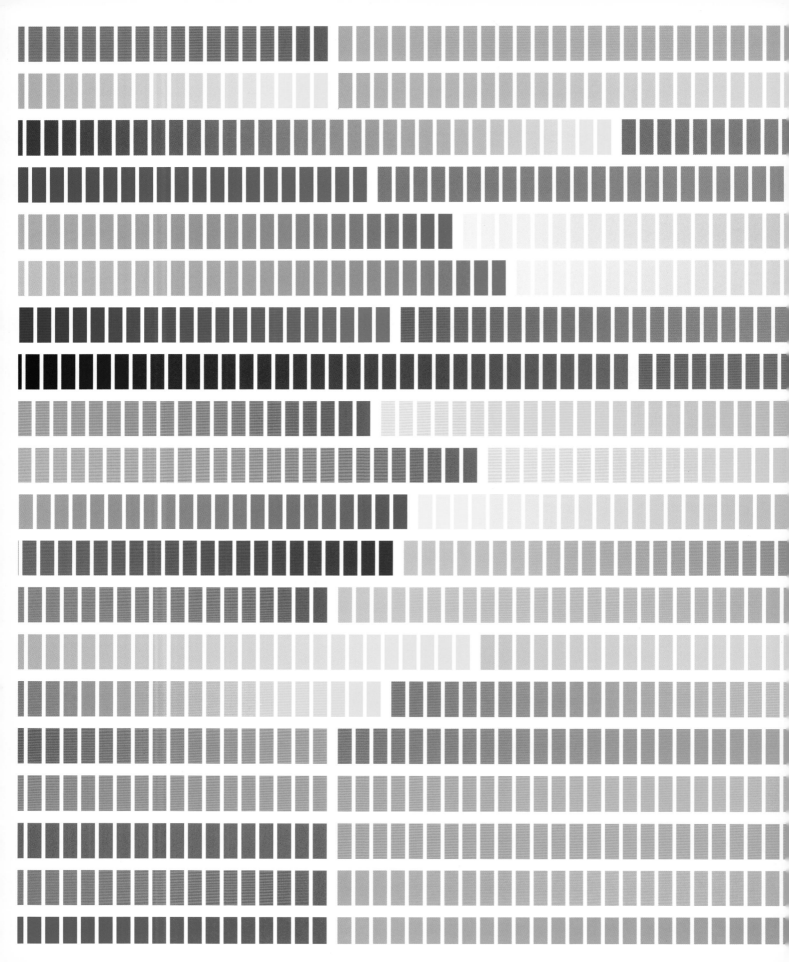

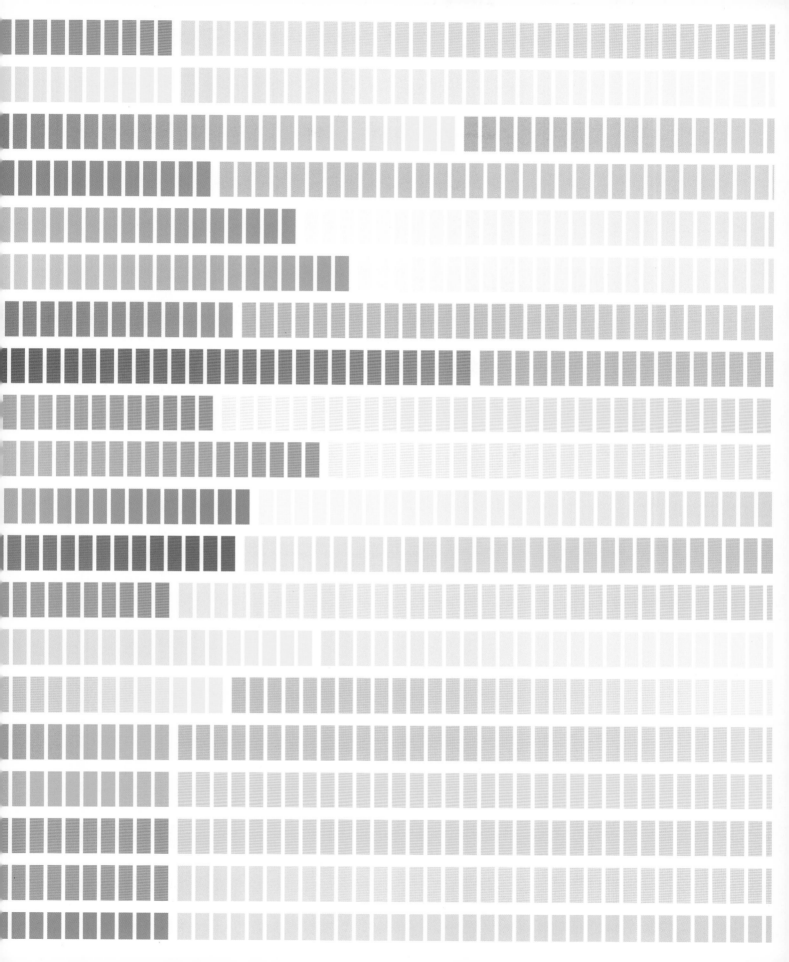

066z

ENSER_3
ROBER PALLÁS

FORMAT **245mm x 295mm**
MATERIAL **CARTRIDGE PAPER_PLASTIC BAG**
TIME_PLACE **2001_SPAIN**

enserhumano@hotmail.com

067z

ENSER_1_THE FAX
ROBER PALLÁS

FORMAT **260mm x 128mm**
MATERIAL **CARTRIDGE PAPER**
TIME_PLACE **2001_SPAIN**

068z

106u_5
ERIC BRAÜN

ILLUSTRATION **SIMON B**
FORMAT **180mm x 215mm**
MATERIAL **FUN FUR_CARTRIDGE PAPER**
TIME_PLACE **1997_CANADA**

069z

BURSTS
**MATTHEW MCCARTHY
AND TONY WARD**

FORMAT **115mm x 165mm**
MATERIAL **PHOTO ALBUM
_FOUND IMAGERY**
TIME_PLACE **1998_AUSTRALIA**

Quote Rober Pallás: **Enser** is a monthly "author fanzine" made with black and white photocopies, which sets out to claim that process as a medium in itself; it's like a laboratory for graphic experimentation. It's also a personal challenge...and a way to have a good time. A restless fanzine, **Enser** changes with each issue and has an external element that gives it personality and differentiates it from other fanzines done with a photocopier; issue two was fastened with an elastic band, which in Spain is known as a "goma de pollo", literally, "chicken rubber", as they're used to fasten dead chickens in the market.

Quote Eric Braün: **106u** in French sounds like "sans issue", which means "no way out". It started off as a way to show my artwork (in French), it became a silent (no words) anthology in 1996, and is now an international art and comix magazine with contributors from around the world, distributed in seven countries! The artwork in **106u** reflects my preference; usually dark, funny and sarcastic pictures and stories. The odd numbered issues have been known to be in a "book-object form", using metal, fur and moulded latex, as experimenting with media is also a concern of mine; and the **106u Virtual Art Comix Museum** is an internet extension. So I want to conquer the world with subversive silent comix from everywhere!!!

A simple and ingenious way to publish a zine, by reusing those cheap, cheesy, photo albums that seem to be given away with every processed film in Australia. Found graphics, from comics, sweet wrappers, swing tags and packaging are either inserted as is, or re-interpreted as black and white or colour photocopies.

070z

PHK_BLUE BAG ISSUE
CINDY HOETMER, DANNY VAN DEN
DUNGEN, MARIEKE STOLK

FORMAT **172mm x 200mm**
MATERIAL **MIXED STOCK_PLASTIC BAG_
CONFECTIONERY_KNICKERS**
TIME_PLACE **1994_THE NETHERLANDS**

071z

PHK_LOWLIFEPUNKSCUM
CINDY HOETMER, DANNY VAN DEN
DUNGEN, MARIEKE STOLK

FORMAT **160mm x 250mm**
MATERIAL **PLASTIC BAG_STICKERS_
POSTER**
TIME_PLACE **1994_THE NETHERLANDS**

072z

PHK_TOFU666
CINDY HOETMER, DANNY VAN DEN
DUNGEN, MARIEKE STOLK

FORMAT **110mm x 150mm**
MATERIAL **CARTRIDGE PAPER_ELASTIC
BAND_STICKERS_PLASTIC BAG**
TIME_PLACE **1995_THE NETHERLANDS**

073z

A-Z ADDRESS BOOK
RYK@MBD

FORMAT **145mm x 95mm**
MATERIAL **MATT PAPER_ELASTIC BAND**
TIME_PLACE **1999_UK_JAPAN**

ryk@mbd.sphere.ne.jp

Quote Cindy Hoetmer, Danny van den Dungen, Marieke Stolk: **PHK** was the zine we published a while ago when we were very much influenced by American zines like Murder Can Be Fun, Drew, Beer Frame, Ben Is Dead, Dishwasher Pete, etc. We wanted to put out a zine ourselves, and so we did. The name **PHK** didn't stand for anything at all, although a lot of people thought it was an abbreviation for "phuk", or "fuck". To make it even more complicated, we, for some strange reasons, usually pronounced PHK as "puke"... so we guess the actual meaning of PHK lies somewhere between phuk and puke...We published exactly four issues of PHK. (Why does it feel like the middle-ages while it was only a few years ago?) Anyway, after that, Danny van den Dungen and Marieke Stolk formed the graphic design studio Experimental Jetset (together with Erwin Brinkers). Cindy Hoetmer went on and became a writer who regularly contributes to magazines and newspapers; her monthly column for the Dutch magazine Blvd is kinda famous.

PHK #1 was basically a plastic zip-lock bag containing various laser-printed stickers and some little booklets.

PHK #2 is the blue square magazine. It contained articles about stuff we found (and, to a certain degree, still find) interesting; other zines, conspiracy theories, urban myths, pop culture, and punk rock.

PHK #3 was again a plastic bag containing stickers and various booklets. This time, the plastic was anti-static material. One of the enclosed booklets was an "all-girl" sub-zine made by Cindy and Marieke called Period.

PHK #4, also called Tofu666, was a little red magazine with a printed cardboard cover. We used a piece of elastic as binding. Again the usual items; conspiracy theories, pop culture and punk rock. Again, we enclosed a bunch of stickers. Two of the inserted stickers were actually contributions by friends: Amsterdam garage band The Slick Mechanics, and befriended zine Grow.

There's also a silk-screened pair of underpants that Marieke designed in an extremely limited run as a **PHK** promotional item.

Whenever we finished an issue, we would organise some kind of "presentation" where people could buy our zine. These events took place in the basement of Amsterdam venue Paradiso. This basement was actually the toilet space. We decorated the place, usually there was a DJ playing noisy music, and one time there was even a band performing live – in the toilet area.

Bound with an elastic band, Ryk's images of vacant urban spaces, obsolete technology and business-like information graphics are interspersed with blank pages providing an even greater sense of emptiness. The whole is held together, just, with an elastic band. Images include: Tesco's car park, Earl's Court, London; road kill; a Playstation advert; Rubik cube; RIBA's women's toilet, London.

074z

UNTITLED
STEPHEN BAKER

FORMAT **115mm x 55mm**
MATERIAL **MIXED STOCK_PLASTIC BAG**
TIME_PLACE **2000_AUSTRALIA**
PUBLISHER **HOUSE**

hugh@sub.net.au

075z

SHIFT!_MEAT/FLESH
ANJA LUTZ AND LILLY TOMEC

FORMAT **210mm x 260mm**
MATERIAL **MIXED STOCK_MEAT HOOK**
TIME_PLACE **1996_GERMANY**

www.shift.de

076z

SHIFT!_HEAT
ANJA LUTZ AND LILLY TOMEC

ILLUSTRATION **OLGA AND PIROGGE_
WEE FLOWERS**
FORMAT **212mm x 260mm**
MATERIAL **MIXED STOCK**
TIME_PLACE **1996_GERMANY**

077z

THE SWITCH_GADGET
NICK BOOTH AND ALEX SMITH

FORMAT **210mm x 297mm**
MATERIAL **CARTRIDGE PAPER**
TIME_PLACE **1996_UK**

Untitled is reminiscent of a home-made cheque book, containing various cut-up printed stock, approximating withdrawal forms for an image bank. The ziplock bag may have contained notes at one time and comes complete with a sticker; Reminder Payment is Overdue.

Each themed issue of **shift!** is compiled from contributions received after a call for entries postcard is distributed to a large mailing list. Then the fun starts, as the format within which the various graphics, illustrations, collage, photography and writing are to appear, imaginatively mirror that theme. Hence Meat/Flesh came wrapped in brown paper punctured with a meat hook; the Heat issue opened like a giant matchbook and the Food issue was printed as a collection of recipe cards housed in a plastic sandwich box, complete with free seeds.

Quote Anja Lutz: Just a few points on why we make **shift!** To experiment; to push the limits of publishing and print; to try out new ways and modes of working and collaborating with people from different disciplines and diverse backgrounds.

Students from Camberwell College of Art introduced real-world objects into layouts for **The Switch**, with the result of intensifying the reader's reaction; hair is taped to a story on barbers and the collapsible binoculars add novelty to the entire issue.

078z

THE SWITCH_HAIR
NICK BOOTH AND ALEX SMITH

FORMAT **210mm x 212mm**
MATERIAL **SCREEN PRINTED COVER_**
CARTRIDGE PAPER_HUMAN HAIR
TIME_PLACE **1996_UK**

079z

TOOT_SEX
SALLY ESSE AND JADE WALSH

FORMAT **130mm x 130mm**
MATERIAL **MIXED STOCK**
TIME_PLACE **2000_AUSTRALIA**

080z

NEW REALITY 2000
HIRO SUGIYAMA

FORMAT **175mm x 85mm**
MATERIAL **METALLIC PRINT_GLOSS PAPER**
TIME_PLACE **2000_JAPAN**
PUBLISHER **ENLIGHTENMENT**

hougado@netjoy.ne.jp

081z

CRAP HOUND_6
SEAN TEJARATCHI

COVER **MARTIN ONTIVEROS**
FORMAT **215mm x 280mm**
MATERIAL **COATED COVER STOCK**
_CARTRIDGE PAPER
TIME_PLACE **1999_USA**

Tons of lovely photocopy experiments, with images reproduced on trace and various coloured stock; the economical one-colour print job on the interior never looks dull due to inventive show-through and some really dense imagery. The whole is held together with an elastic band and a wrap-around jacket.

Intoxicatingly overlapped line art, mixing flora and fauna, sports, religious figures, furniture, sculpture and technology from an age when imagery was a much simpler concern than today. Metallic ink and papers combine to create pattern and texture; presented in a delicate slipcase.

In case you were wondering, ambiguity is probably this issue's Big Theme. All three topics (death, telephones and scissors) exhibit the shifting associations and conflicting functions common to the widespread and useful. With regards to death, though, its philosophic yin and yang have already been at the center of a thousand clichés. I feel we can safely skip that, blahblahblah....Let's move on to phones, shall we? Telephones embody ambiguity on a much more personal and immediate level. The ringing of a phone in the middle of the night has never been a comforting sound...answering one has always been a bit like reaching blindly into a black box and hoping for something that won't bite....I love scissors because they provide a tiny glimpse into the need for selective destruction. They're essentially destructive tools that have somehow been classed as creative. This might seem rather obvious and unworthy of discussion, but consider the widespread pressure to eradicate negativity from every corner of one's life. I've personally lost count of the dead-end conversations I've had with those who like to "focus on the positive", and confide in soothing tones that "negativity only brings you down, man"...

Many images in **Crap Hound** have copyrights held by various lawsuit-friendly entities. Remember that **Crap Hound** is scathing social commentary and emphatically not a collection of images with which to trample the fragile rights of huge corporations. **Crap Hound** officially urges you to obey all laws, all the time, and encourages abject submission to anyone with money and law on their side.

082z

LOVE
CHRIS LOVE

FORMAT **148.5mm x 210mm**
MATERIAL **UNCOATED PAPER**
TIME_PLACE **2001_UK**
PUBLISHER **GOG MOGOG**

mysterycatt@hotmail.com
gog.magog@virgin.net

Quote Chris Love: The zine is something I have to do, it's an urge and is about spreading love and an exploration of what I think love is. We need more love in the world, and everyone should interpret love in their own way.

083z

DIE-CUT PLUG WIRING DIAGRAMS
MARK PAWSON

FORMAT **70mm x 70mm**
MATERIAL **CARTRIDGE PAPER_COTTON**
TIME_PLACE **1994_REVISED 1999_UK**

www.mpawson.demon.co.uk

Mark Pawson makes various paper publications at regular intervals and also runs a zines and artists' book distribution operation called Disinfotainment c/o, PO Box 664, London, E3 4QR, that distributes many zines via an extensive mailing list.

Quote Mark Pawson: I'm an image junkie, I make books to keep myself amused and ward off the encroachment of consensus reality. (On e-zines) I'm more impressed if someone makes a paper zine than a website – I could make three sites right now this afternoon, but a zine takes a lot more effort and nothing beats the tactile quality of paper.

084z

CANNIBALS OF NORTH AMERICA
JULIETTE TORREZ

ILLUSTRATION **SCOTT MILLS**
FORMAT **105mm x 140mm**
MATERIAL **COLOURED PAPERS_STICKER**
TIME_PLACE **2000_USA**
PUBLISHER **KAPOW!**

kapowbooks@chickmail.com

A finely produced travelogue of a USA road trip combining words and illustrations. The careful choice of papers and a vintage-y sticker look as if they may have been collected on the way.

085z

MAD WOMAN'S BREAKFAST
LIZ WAKEFIELD

FORMAT **245mm x 173mm**
MATERIAL **WALLPAPER_PLASTIC FLOWERS_COLOURED PAPER_ GOLD THREAD**
TIME_PLACE **2001_UK**

Liz Wakefield was prompted to start zine-ing during a **GirlFrenzy** night of music and mayhem at Brighton's Sanctuary Cafe. After contributing to a number of titles she took the plunge herself and began documenting life as a working mother of two growing kids, with a houseful of creative projects. Preoccupations include drawing, wrestling (as a spectator) and John Peel.

086z

HEADBONE
HITCH

FORMAT **75mm x 107mm**
MATERIAL **COATED PAPER
_NEWSPAPER**
TIME_PLACE **1990_UK**
PUBLISHER **PETALPRESS**

jmhitchen@hotmail.com

Graphic designer and animator Hitch
experiments with different paper and print
techniques in a mini-zine full of his
characteristically bizarre creatures.

087z

INFILTRATION
NINJ

FORMAT **140mm x 205mm**
MATERIAL **CARTRIDGE PAPER**
TIME_PLACE **1997-1999_CANADA**

Infiltration is remarkable for presenting an
unapologetically niche and obsessive
subject matter. It's all about breaking the
law, i.e. trespassing, so as to investigate
the mysteries of defunct landscapes and
institutions; from beached wrecks to
missile silos and abandoned schools; in
the name of unabashed adventure. The
resultant photography and well-drawn
diagrammatics of places most of us would
never have the nerve to stray into, are
fascinating. Its do-it-yourself, anti-
establishment stance is perfectly echoed in
the no-nonsense, black and white, stapled
zine format.

088z

REVERSE WORLD
HIRO SUGIYAMA

FORMAT **80mm x 115mm**
MATERIAL **COLOUR PHOTOCOPIES**
TIME_PLACE **1997_JAPAN**
PUBLISHER **ENLIGHTENMENT**

hougado@netjoy.ne.jp

Sharp juxtapositions of intense colour
shots, showing everyday life in Japan, in
detail, cut-up and under the microscope.
Even the ink's smell is too intense!

089z

LEFTSIDE_DRAFT 2
LEFTSIDE DESIGN

PHOTOGRAPHY **KYN AND CAI TAYLOR**
ILLUSTRATION **STEVE JOHNSTONE**
FORMAT **240mm x 280mm**
MATERIAL **UNCOATED PAPER**
TIME_PLACE **2000_UK**

leftsidedesign@hotmail.com

Typographic experimentations, next to
photography, illustration, writing and
assemblage; **Leftside** offers an open call
for contributions. Those who responded to
draft 2 include; Kieran O'Connor, Austen
Aggrey, Tommy Evans, Atsushi Hasegawa,
Louise Foley, James Welch, Tim Ellis, Andy
Williams, Justine Belcher, Sarah Elizabeth
Watters, Simon Thompson, Steve Johnston,
Samantha Harley, Shane Gullen. Their
contributions are treated to some fairly
energetic design treatments.

Remember there are no rules, what you
do is entirely up to you but have fun and
be passionate.

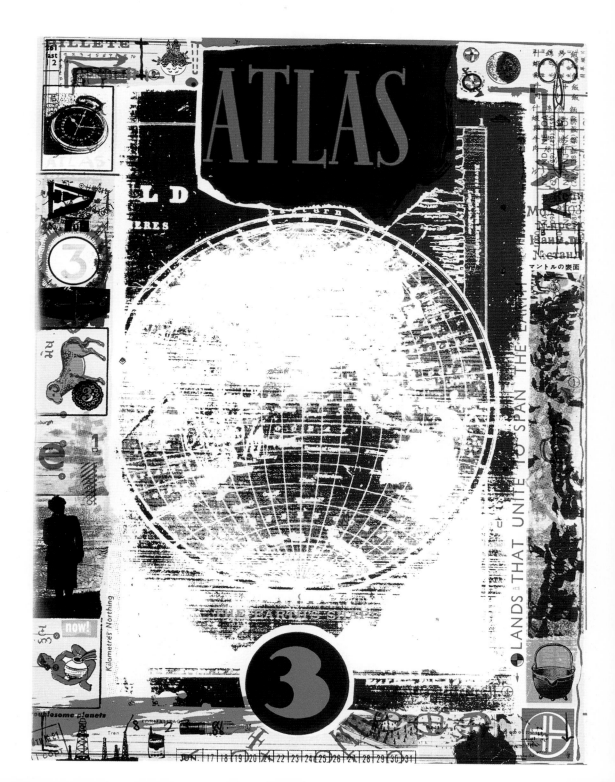

GONZO

BINGO

B	I	N	G	O
13	21	43	55	69
14	25	44	48	61
12	16	FREE 1674 SPACE	52	63
11	23	31	49	71
3	29	40	56	66

[N⁰] 646 1674

003z

X-mas in Woody Creek

I set a trap in the chimney for Santa Claus last night, but all I caught was a huge skunk with rabies.

It taught me a harsh lesson about God & the way he works: Never use hooks on dry land.

They don't call those dumb bastards "fish" for nothing, & skunks can't live under water.

It also taught me, once again, that Santa Claus is a liar. He skips many houses & he cheats a lot of children. He never said he didn't have a few cruel Jokes in his bag — but putting a skunk down my chimney was over the the line. That was crazy.

December 25, 2000

HUNTER S. THOMPSON

X-RAY BOOK CO.

THROW AWAY THE TRASH CAN

Volkswagon memories
Tipping from tippling
Boots dangling from
A Del Playa Cliffside.
maudlin as hell
knocking off small rocks
with my heel
until I have
Something to
stand on.

Brook Dalton

31/100

the next
cactus
brief

(will be with

(you very soon

Identification

contempt

précieux
es étu

cactus firework

stu

This issue 13 will be the last
edition of cactus produced in
we have decided that in future a magazine
would make it easier for people in the
get involved, and enable a wider audience
to see your work.

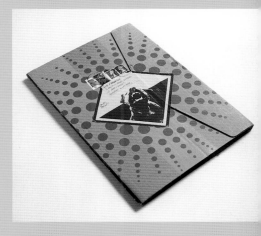

GUILTY

Mustang
MS.
GTO
MUSCLE
America

gunfight 29

figure : issue : seven

gunfight

maki...
to da... ay and

15 ¶ ... the children of ... cried unto Pharaoh, ... efore dealest thou thus ... thy servants?

16 There is no straw given unto thy servants, and they say to us, Make brick: and, behold, thy servants *are* beaten; but the fault *is* in thine own people.

17 But he said, Ye *are* idle, *ye are* idle: therefore ye say, Let us go *and* do sacrifice to the LORD.

18 Go therefore now, *and* work; for there shall no straw be given you, yet shall ye deliver the tale of bricks.

19 And the officers of the children of Israel did see *that* they *were* in evil *case*, after it was said, Ye shall not minish *ought* from your bricks of your daily task.

20 ¶ And they met Moses and Aaron, who stood in the way, as they came forth from Pharaoh:

21 And they said unto them, The LORD look upon you, and judge; because ye have made our savour to be abhorred in the eyes of Pharaoh, and in the eyes of his servants, to put a sword in their hand to slay us.

22 And ... unto the LORD, a... wherefore hast the... ated this people? ... thou hast sent me...

23 For ... haraoh to speak in ... ath done evil to ... ther hast thou del... e at all.

THEN ... unto Moses, Now shalt thou see what I will do to Pharaoh: for with a strong hand shall he let them go, and with a strong hand shall he drive them out of his land.

40 Thou shalt be over my house, and according unto thy word shall all my people be ruled: only in the throne will I be greater than thou.

41 And Pharaoh said unto Joseph, See, I have set thee over all the land of Egypt.

42 And Pharaoh took off his ring from his hand, and put it upon Joseph's hand, and arrayed him in vestures of fine linen, and put a gold chain about his neck;

43 And he made him to ride in the second chariot which he had; and they cried before him, Bow the knee: and he made him *ruler* over all the land of Egypt.

44 And Pharaoh said unto Joseph, I *am* Pharaoh, and without thee shall no man lift up his hand or foot in all the land of Egypt.

45 And Pharaoh called Joseph's name Zaphnath-paaneah; and he gave him to wife Asenath...

...seven good ears... the dream *is* one.

27 And the seven thin and ill favoured kine that came up after them *are* seven years; and the seven empty ears blasted with the east wind shall be seven years of famine.

28 This *is* the thing which I have spoken unto Pharaoh: What God *is* about to do he sheweth unto Pharaoh.

29 Behold, there come seven years of great plenty throughout all the land of Egypt:

30 And there shall arise after them seven years of famine; and all the plenty shall be forgotten in the land of Egypt; and the famine shall consume the land;

31 And the plenty shall not be known in the land by reason of that famine following: for it *shall* be very grievous.

32 And for that the dream was...

And I will be found of you, saith the LORD: and I will turn away your captivity, and I will gather you from all the nations, and from all the places whither I have driven you, saith the LORD; and I will bring you again into the place whence I caused you to be carried away captive.

¶ Because ye have said, The LORD hath raised us up prophets in Babylon;

¶ ... that thus saith the LORD ...

¶ Thus saith the LORD of the house of David ...

... Because they have committed villany in Israel, and have committed adultery with their neighbours' wives, and have spoken lying words in my name, which I have not commanded them; even I know, and am a witness, saith the LORD.

¶ And ... thou shalt also speak ... Shemaiah the Nehelamite, saying ...

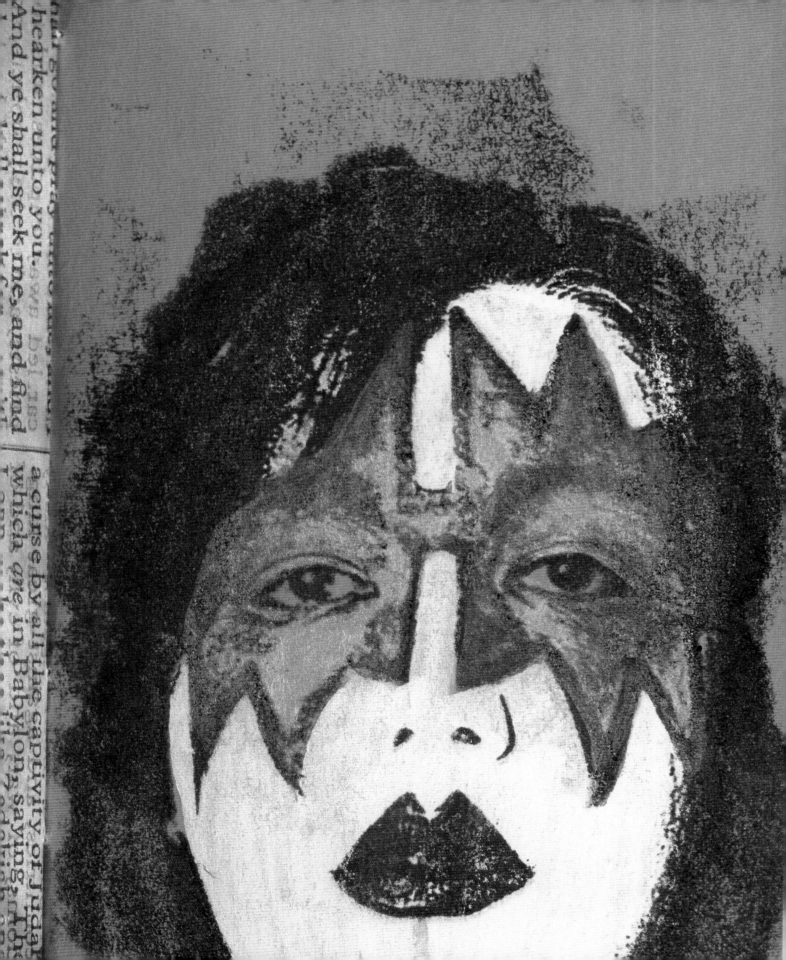

PETROLEUM SPIRIT OF THE NATION

NHS

5. Don't burn your fingers by allowing people to die because fuel shortages are affecting hospitals.

6. Let it die down and give the government a 60 days ultimatum to lower the fuel tax.

MP MP PM MP MP

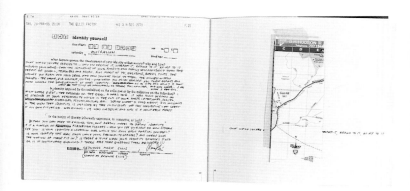

011z

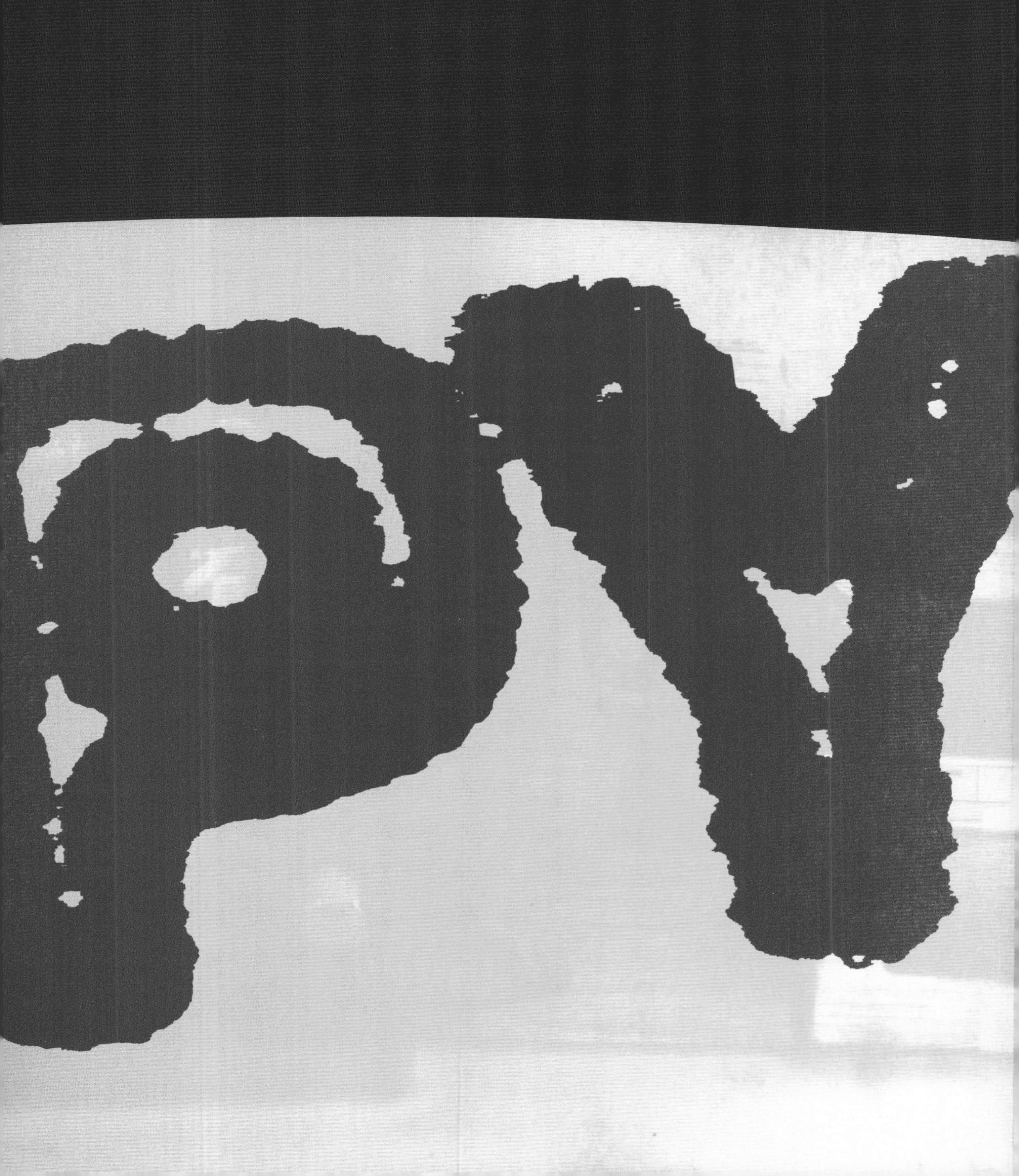

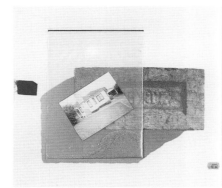

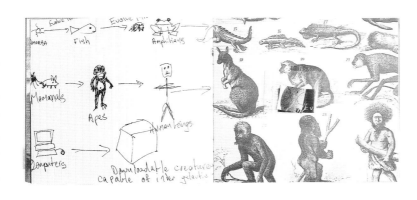

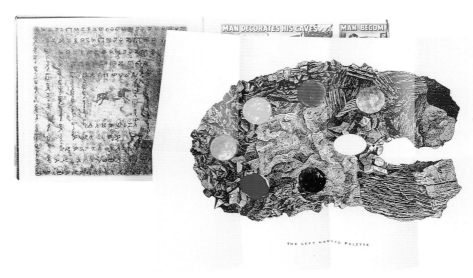

In different prison camps in Italy.

But, with great good fortune, they were brought again in Rome where they managed to gain asylum i Vatican. This was in September 1943. Here they b stay until after the fall of Rome in June 1944.

Larkin and his companion were in the same operati Tripoli and they, too, were taken prisoner. Howev were lucky enough to escape from their captors within hours.

Doc. Thomson refers with considerable satisfacti much-improved organisation at Brixham as compared

112

don't
panic

014z

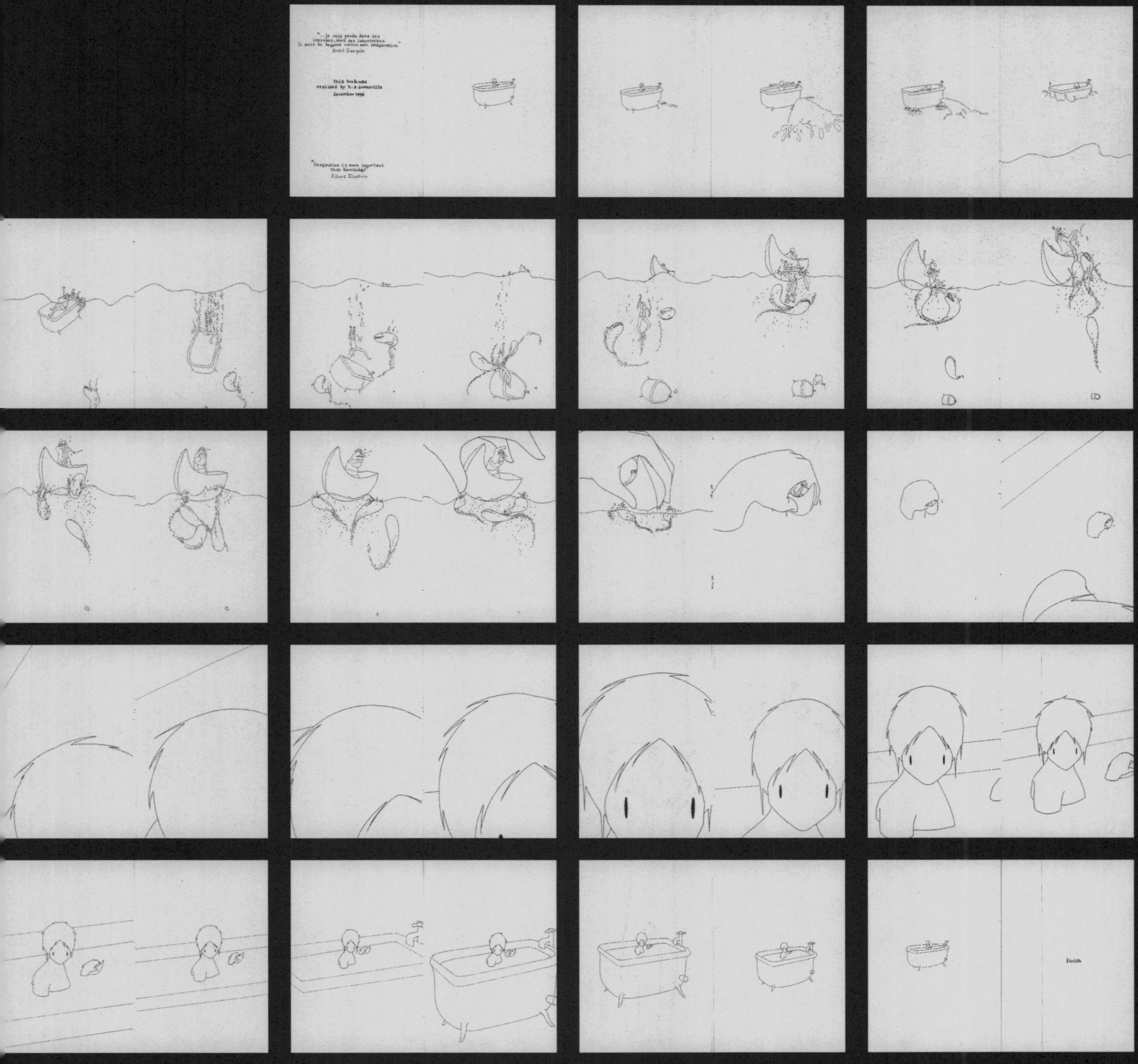
this book was
realised by h.s.somerville
december 1996
"Imagination is more important
than knowledge"
Albert Einstein
finish

click

cret
ON BASE

PROJECT JOSHUA

We have already been to

MARS

A
is the name of the moon base sighted and filmed by the Apollo astonauts.

ase

ally yours.

alternative3 **3.**

OMPANIES

EBE **PROJECT** **GRUDGE**

extraterrestrial biolog i cal en

contains
16 volumes
of information
collected
from the
beginning of
United States
nvestigation of
unidentified
flying
objects (UFOs)
and
identified
n crafts (IACs)

excalibur underground bases
a weapon to destroy the alien

the

ook

re-educate
disinformation
educational deterioration

hor chin

The government
of the
United States
was confronted
with a series
of events which
were to change
beyond prediction
its future and
with it the future
of humanity.

issued an ultimatum to MJ12

THE PRESIDENT
was going to go
public

with the truth about the drugs and the alie

truth is believing

n body parts
were found inside
16 **crashed or downed**
65 alien bodies

and 1 live alien

Gre
THE PRESIDENT'S BRAIN
alien crafts
a s s a s s i n a

secret service

They will de...

#902447

CIA ASSASSINATIONS

Today
cities exist o
populate...

which makes regular trips into space

a craft that exists at Area 51

Throughout our history, the aliens
have man...

AURORA

**area
s-4**

TAV

Aliens have be...
race thro...
throughout the...
religion, ...
project AQUA...
and the o...

TRANSATMOSPHERIC VEHICLE

The Bilderbergers have evolved into a
secret world government
that now controls almost everything.
The United Nations is a...

Bilderbergers

inte...

control the world

The Bilderbergers are trying to establish a one world government and
economic system sontrolled by them only for their own private utopia.

1 out of every 40 people in the United States

has bee...

Our intelligence services have learned cloning techniques

thought *transmissions*

from the Zeta Reticulan Grey aliens
who use cloning for reproduction of their species.
The shadow government can

pub...

OWN YOUR MIND

clone anyone
clone

clone

to create controlled beings.

Alien

to oversee and conduct all covert
activities concerned with

COMMITTEE

also have the abilit...

the alien question

The secret government has set u...

5412

national sec...

dulce rep...

UNDERGROUND LAB

no commen...

Every major law enforcement center has a telephone
number that they are

...APPEARED.

to call if they find bodies

mutilated in a specific

manner.

guests

aliens exchanged for

humans who gav...

o   n

ordered by the MJ12

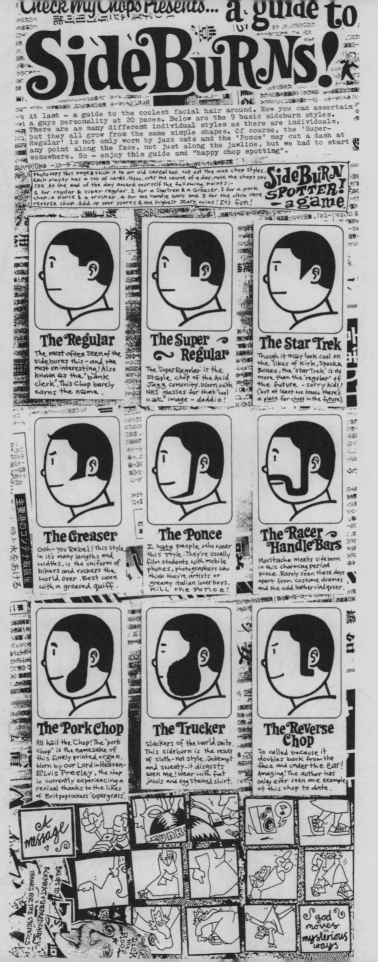

Check My Chops Presents... a guide to SideBurns!

At last - a guide to the coolest facial hair around. Now you can assertain a guys personality at 20 paces. Below are the 9 basic sideburn styles. There are as many different individual styles as there are individuals, but they all grow from the same simple shapes. Of course, the 'Super-Regular' is not only worn by jazz cats and the 'Ponce' may cut a dash at any point along the face, not just along the jawline, but we had to start somewhere. So - enjoy this guide and "happy chop spotting".

SideBurn SPOTTER! - a game

Photo copy this page & stick it to an old cereal box, cut out the nine chop styles. Each player has a set of cards. Now, over the course of a day, note the chops you see. At the end of the day award yourself the following points:-
1 for regular & super regular. 2 for a Star Trek & a Greaser. 3 for a pork chop, a ponce & a trucker. 4 for the handle bars and 5 for the ultra rare reverse chop. Add up your scores & the highest score wins! It's fun!

The Regular
The most often seen of the sideburns this - and the most uninteresting! Also known as the 'bank clerk'. This Chop barely earns the name.

The Super Regular
The Super Regular is the staple chop of the Acid Jazz comunity. Worn with NHS glasses for that 'cool cat' image - daddio!

The Star Trek
Though it may look cool on the likes of Kirk, Spock & Bones, the 'star Trek' is no more than the 'regular' of the future - sorry kids! (but at least we knows there's a place for chops in the future).

The Greaser
Ooh - You Rebel! This style in it's many lengths and widths, is the uniform of bikers and rockers the world over. Best worn with a greased quiff.

The Ponce
I hate people who wear this style. They're usually film students with mobile phones, photographers who think they're artists or greasy italian lover boys. KiLL the Ponce!

The Racer Handle Bars
Moustache meets sideburn in this charming period piece. Rarely seen these days apart from costume dramas and the odd leather-clad queer.

The Pork Chop
All hail the 'Chop! The 'pork chop" is the namesake of this finely printed organ. Worn by our Lord in Heaven - ELvis Presley, the chop is currently experiencing a revival thanks to the likes of Britpoprockers 'supergrass'.

The Trucker
slackers of the world unite. This sideburn is the result of sloth - not style. Unkempt and sweaty - it disgusts even me! Wear with fat jowls and egg stained shirt.

The Reverse Chop
So called because it doubles back from the face and under the ear! Amazing! The author has only ever seen one example of this chop to date.

A message

god moves in mysterious ways

DOLLY BADGE

PLEASE SHUT UP MADAME!
ISSUE TWO: AUTUMN 1997

A ZINE MADE BY BORED TELEPHONE OPERATORS

EDITOR: KAREN ELIOT
LAYOUT: SOME GEEK

NO ADVERTISING
NO SUBSCRIPTIONS
NO DEADLINES
NO PERFUME INSERTS

He Said, She Said
Lypsinka Live Review
By Shawna Virago

Recently, the latest and greatest royal couple of San Francisco, the debonair Don Davenport and myself, graced Josie's Cabaret and Juice Joint for Lypsinka's farewell performance in our lavender little town. Lypsinka has it all, from confidence and cosmetics to petite size 13 shoes, and she was simply fabu that entire evening, but the night, the glamour, the fans were eating out of our french manicured hands! What can I say, except it's true!

The famous photographers and talent scouts were clamoring to give me their cards as well as vouchers to the casting couch. "Shawna," one of the scouts said, "a star says yes, and a starlet thinks it over."

"Are you able to use a noun and a verb?"

Anyway, Don was just a perfect gentleman (he even wore a necktie!) and picked me up in the glass-domed Davenport-mobile, and like any post- apocalyptic gal worth her bath salt, this kitten was ready to rock and dressed to cause cardiac arrest, wearing nothing but a black bra, black Donna Karan tights and cherry leather cowgirl hot pants; I finshed off the outfit with my five-inch kick boxing stilettos. I like my men covered up but the bare-it-all-and-believe-it look is for me.

Please don't get me wrong: I love Lypsinka and I think it's fair to say we're mutual fans of each other and it was never my intent to upstage her, but dammit Lippy! Don't hate me because I am tall and sexier than a young Shelley Frabres! From the moment we arrived at Josie's and were shown our seats by the cute, young, host slaveboy, all eyes were upon us and especially me. I could feel all their eyes undressing me and hopefully they were spanking or flogging me very hard in their dirty little minds.

Don promptly ordered a beer and I told the cute Josie's slaveboy waiter to "Bring me a cocktail, but hold the 'tail." The lights went down and old pro Lippy came out and gave her little orphan andy best. Sadly, that little aura of excitement the crowd was feeding on was coming from our table and if puffy eyes could kill, Miss Lippy's eyes would have bored a hole clean through my skull (which I'm glad they didn't because Don is a horny dog around skull orafices and he would've messed up my Nancy Sinatra fall). Anyways, Lippy was working the stage trying to take the hearts of the crowd back, but it only had the effect of making her appear like Ernest Borgnine in a bad action piece, running amok after a bad enema experience outtake from the Poseidon Adventure. No, the glamour, the glitter were ours.

"Chew your food while I put you on hold, and then we'll talk."

Don wasn't feeling well, something about his snazzy new shoes being too tight, so he spent the night first crawling around on his knees under our table being naughty with the tourists and then finally passing out in stall number one in the ladies room. While he was in the loo, some straight guy asked me if I was a member of the Swedish Bikini Team which pissed me off because, unlike them, I'm a natural blonde and dropped my pants right there to prove it, which was a big mistake since the clown began howling like a wolfchild at full moon. Also, I would have thrown my Shirley Temple right in his hamburger-like face but I pulled back, telling myself that Mary Tyler Moore would not approve (it's true that's the only commandment that ever workd for me, well, I also never covet my neighbor's oxen...), so I spared the bum. But Poor Lippy! The old trooper stormed off the stage only to trip over a drunken Don Davenport who had somehow managed to crawl in between exit stage right and the green room. With her wig and false lashes flying akimbo, Don still had the calm to ask her for an autograph, and like a real pro she complied.

After security took the wolfboy away, Lippy, Don and I went back to Don's swank pad and had a full-on starch party, consuming box after box of potato buds, Carnation instant milk, and plates of Hostess products. Until next time, remember, I love all the children.

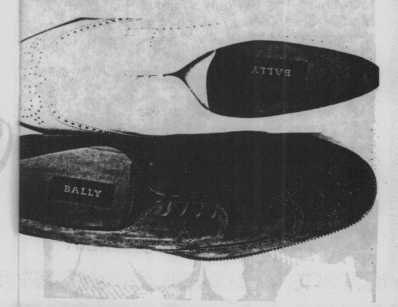

)o you
like

n't

ıen

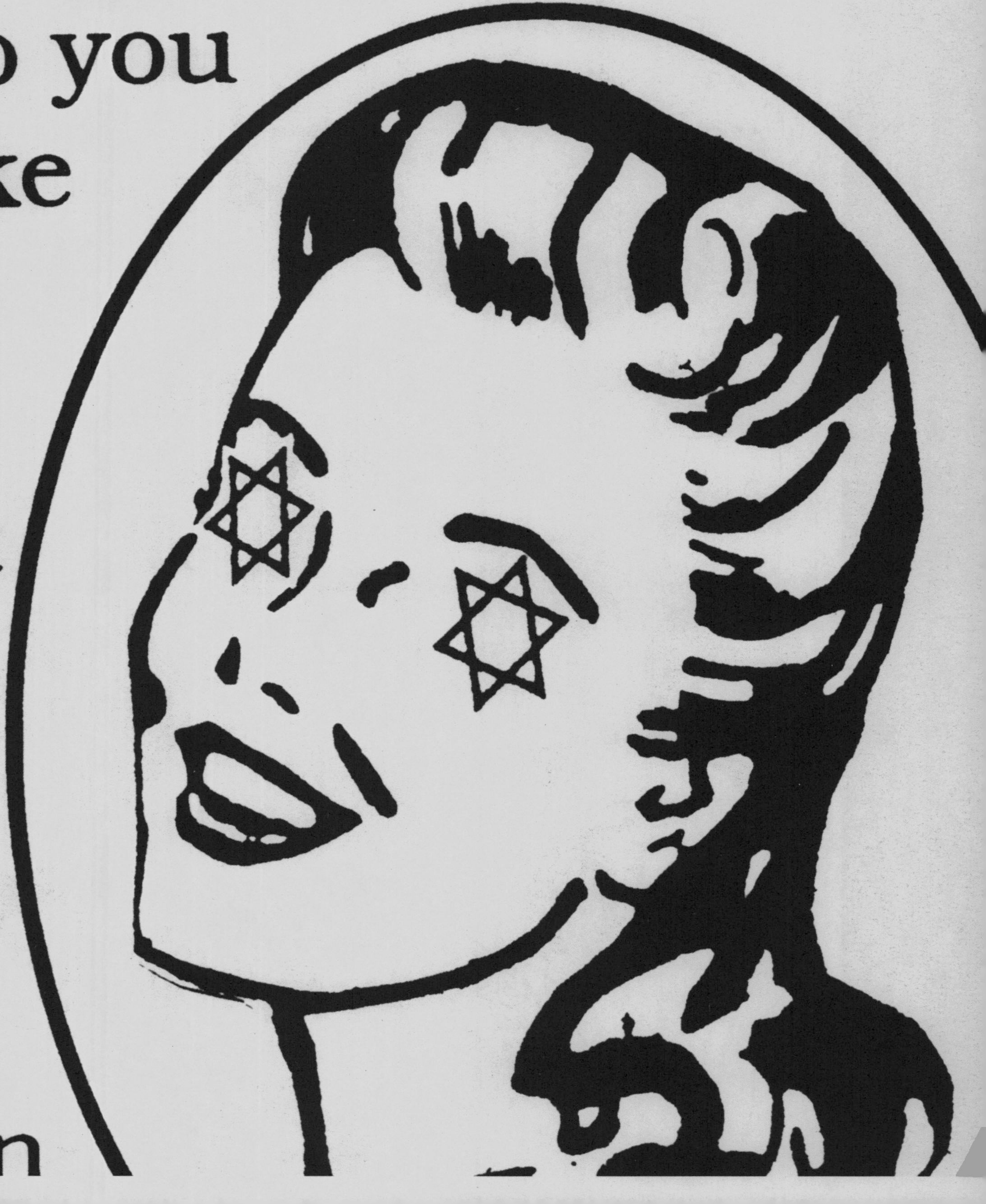

TV
PLOTZ

Issue #15
$2.$00

TV LISTINGS for the fachadded.

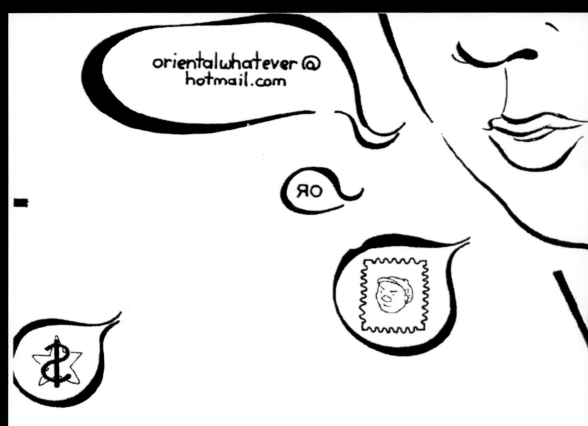

orientalwhatever @
hotmail.com

ORIENTAL WHATEVER
BOX 24
520 FREDERICK ST.
SAN FRANCISCO,CA
94117

TO:

ISSUE #7 $3.00

ORIENTAL WHATEVER

JAPANIZE 4

£1   #

QUIM

SIN OH

EV ET   MO D

UK OF GB
AND NI

by
TOKO

PASSPORT

20.5.99

JAPANIZE

2   £1.50

MASUMI

See...
I brought your magazine in New York and I have to tell you it really
got my dick hard.

Thankyou very much indeed,
Wayne Daniel, New Jersey, USA.

BY
TOKO

£1.5

JAPANIZE
#8

The CHAP
ISSUE 7 £1.50

CADDING ABOUT
HAT DOFFING
DADA DEPILATION
PIPE SIGNALLING

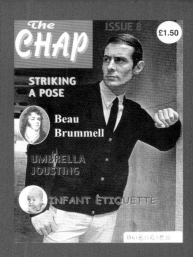

The CHAP
ISSUE 8 £1.50

STRIKING A POSE
Beau Brummell
UMBRELLA JOUSTING
INFANT ETIQUETTE

The CHAP
ISSUE 5 £1.50

JOHN WATERS
THE TRUTH ABOUT SMOKING
CONSUMPTIVE COSMETICS
THE SEMIOTICS OF DRINKING

The CHAP
ISSUE 9 £1.75

MODERN ART
Daniil Kharms
The Semiotics of Footwear
PORTION CONTROL

Howard Spent investigates

THE SEMIOTICS OF DRINKING

Some years ago now, in the heady days that might loosely be referred to as my 'youth', to my eternal shame I used to frequent one of the more louche drinking holes in the heart of Soho. Of all the soiled and tragic habitués of this resort, one member of the throng sticks in my mind to this day. Unfortunately, I never discovered his name but his essence still haunts my soul to its innermost core. As a budding observer of the human condition, his attitude struck me at once as epitomising the triumph of laconicism over adversity. Constantly in a state of alcoholic ineptitude, he would wander about the pub enunciating but one intelligible word. That word was "Shostakovich". It seems that through the course of a cultured and no doubt rich life, this fellow, faced with impending alcoholism had gradually condensed his entire existence, with its aspirations and triumphs, into a simple four syllable expression. To some this may have seemed a failure, but to me it represented an achievement close to Zen enlightenment. The masterful selection of one sibilant word, easily pronounceable in a state of advanced intoxication but at the same time of high cultural value, singled him out as a fellow journeyman of erudition and panache.

This is but one example that the squalid world of drinking has to offer, of how complex meaning can be condensed into a brief readable form known as semiotics.

Striding manfully into any place of adult refreshment, one only needs an ounce or two of perspicacity and the eyes in one's head to read the truth of people's lives merely through the way they act. In case you lack either of these qualities, dear reader, there follows a brief summary of my own observations that represents the result of many gruelling months of laborious field work, propping up bars in highly disreputable venues, chatting to ladies of questionable virtue and quaffing stunning quantities of virulent liquor. My suffering is your gain. I humbly offer you the fruits of my labour.

Read and gain insight, for quite rightly did Pliny the Elder pen the eternal words 'In vino veritas'. I exhort you to absorb and memorise these pages for use socially, in business and for pleasure.

The Sublime
The man who throws his life and soul open to malt whisky, undiluted and sans glace, is a man of rare distinction and impeccable character. More a religious vocation than a drink, ancient malt ordains its imbiber as the heir to dionysus's sacred mantel.

The Vulgarian
This demented guttersnipe obviously thinks that he is hip and with-it to drink foreign lager straight out of the bottle. Such an assumption is as sickening as it is wrong-headed. He richly deserves a good thrashing and a savage kick in the billingsgate.

The Connoisseur
This ludicrous looking fellow might know a thing or two about vintages, tails and chocolatey aromas but appearing too finickity and fastidious has never been, and never will be, calculated to win the hearts of ladies. Expertise is often the mask of impotence.

The Arriviste
A glass filled with a lurid concoction, piled high with fruit and novelty items singles, this man out as a social inferior who imagines that distinction and caché can be bought by the ounce. His profession in sales is wholly incompatible with being a gentleman.

The Lovers
Sweethearts in the first flush of romance are liable to throw all caution to the wind and attempt risky manoeuvres involving drinking whilst linking arms. Such moves are highly foolhardy, may result in serious injury and in rare cases can prove fatal.

The Real Ale Man

There is no shame for a man of sensibility and sophistication to indulge, on occasions, in an honest pint or twelve. By imbibing malty brews and guffawing loudly, this fellow gains the common touch, and, thus, the respect and trust of the hoi polloi.

The Serious Drinker

A slight over dependence on the stimulating effects of gin are not a worrying matter, but more a sign of generosity of spirit, and a robust and forthright approach to life. This fellow's highly admirable behaviour makes him a prince among men.

The Deviant

The 15th Earl of Camardenshire's colossal fortune and rather outré temperament might legitimize his theatrical tastes in clothing, but nothing can possibly excuse his drinking of 80's embrocations with names such as 'Taboo', 'Mirage' or 'Zapatista'.

The Tankardeers

Although they are unrelated, Robert and Julian have developed a deep and trusting father-and-son relationship. Their bonding has been helped by a shared love of pewter tankards and frequent cultural vacations to louche resorts on the coast of Morocco.

The Senior Man

To the civilised man about town, indecision as to what to drink should never present a problem. At all times of the day the noble Martini can be regarded as a haven in a fickle and turbulent world. Sexual gratification at this man's hands is virtually guaranteed.

The Under-aged

Sometimes it can be difficult for a publican or owner of an off-license to spot an under-age drinker attempting to flout the law. This young turk dupes his adversaries by the fiendish ruse of donning a frighteningly convincing facial appendage.

The Plainly Ridiculous

"Sir, there seems to be an extraneous object in the neck of my bottle. Kindly remove it at once". This imported affectation leaves a right-minded fellow irate and perplexed, and is merely designed to disguise the lamentable taste of the lager within.

The Artist

It has long been a tradition among artists and so-called 'creative' people to imbibe cheap but stylish drinks such as Absinthe, Thunderbird and Creosote. Despite ceaseless mythologising about the dangers of such beverages, there is no evidence of long term harm.

CHILDREN-OUTDOOR ACTIVITIES

209915   AL HAMDAN

MY FIRST CAR!!!

BY NURSE RATCHET

THE AMAZING TRUE STORY OF A TRUCKIE WITH TWO ARSEHOLES

Graham was a 30 year old truck driver admitted to my hospital for surgical repair of his anal fistula. In other words, he had developed a 'second bum'. A doctor would correctly call this disease pilonidal sinus but my term of endearment for this unfortunate condition was 'trucker's arsehole'. Why you may ask? Because of the incredible number of truck drivers admitted every year with similar symptoms, not all of whom are half as bad as Graham. It was first noted during WWII and was originally labelled 'jeep riders' disease. So Graham is not alone. In fact, 77,000 Service-men were hospitalised for the problem which accounted for 4.2 million sick days. There aren't so many jeeps around in the 21st century but there are a lot of trucks. The theory: constant sitting in bumpy vehicles for long periods of time drove neighbouring hair ends into other hair follicles (the shaft from which hair comes from) causing a severe inflammatory response. A small infection would ensue creating an abscess, which will often rupture inwards, driving the infection further into the tissue, creating what is known in the trade as a fistula. Worst case scenarios end up like our dear truckie friend Graham. The infection extends so deeply that it can perforate the browneye. Graham didn't know which hole to wipe, which one was responsible for the smell or which sphincter to clench if a Roo ran out in front of his Big Rig. On a positive note, Graham found that with practice he could fart in stereo and as he said to me later "at least I don't have dual sets of haemorrhoids!". Best thing is to prevent it because they do have a tendency to become chronic problems. Keep your arse dry and clean as a whistle, curse your mum if you've inherited the hairy crack gene and in general keep a close eye on your coit. And if you develop truckers arse, lets hope that you're not too anal to seek help and pray like hell the doctor isn't a bum bandit looking for a date.

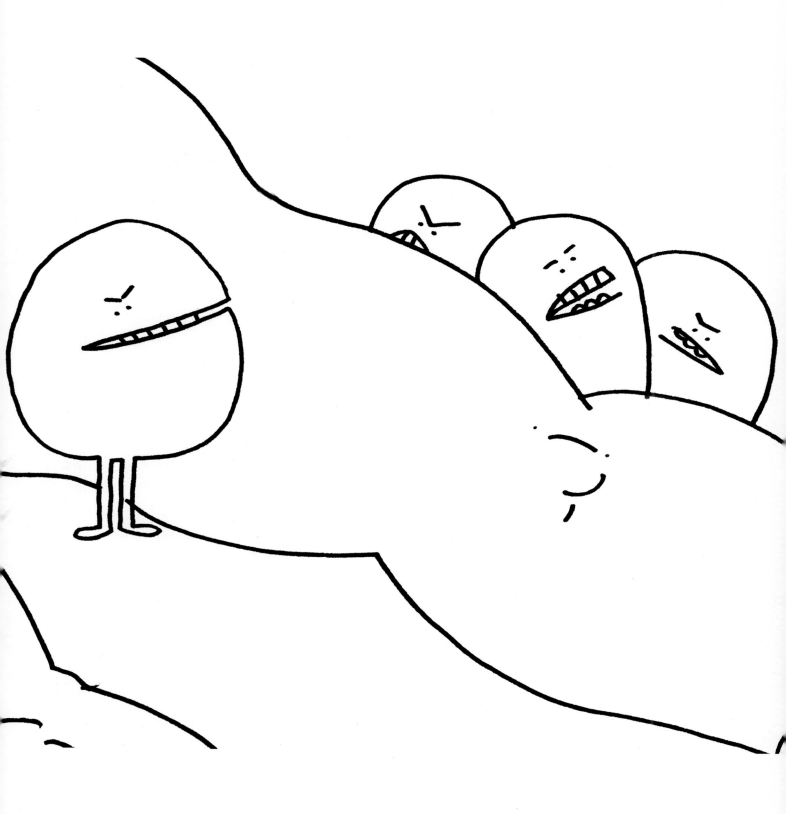

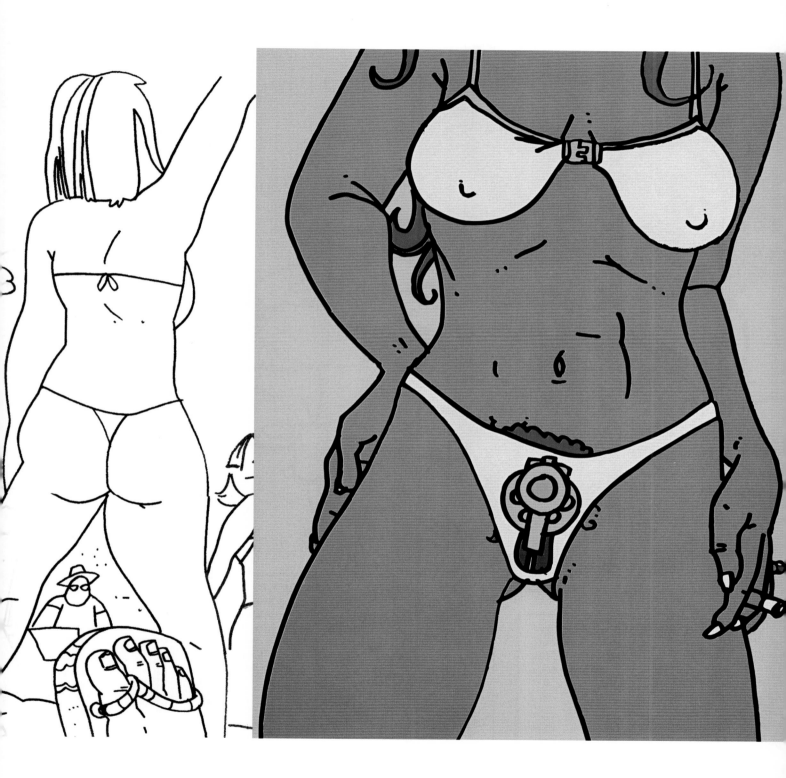

important: use the silent language

If you had a gadget

STEP 1: For this experiment you will need the following:
• 44 milligrams of Sodium Prophide
• 2 beakers of Disalvic Acid
• 8 mili-liters of Hydrochloric Benzine

STEP 2: Carefully combine all elements in a **beaker** and heat over a **bunsen burner** for 1 minute.

STEP 3: Carry the **beaker** to a classroom window and take one final look out at the sky. Bring the **beaker** to your lips and drink.

STEP 4: Fall to the floor **dead**. That will show them all. Every last one of them. They **never understood** you. They **never cared**. Now that your miserable life is over, they can all live with **your death** forever, with **nobody to blame but themselves**.

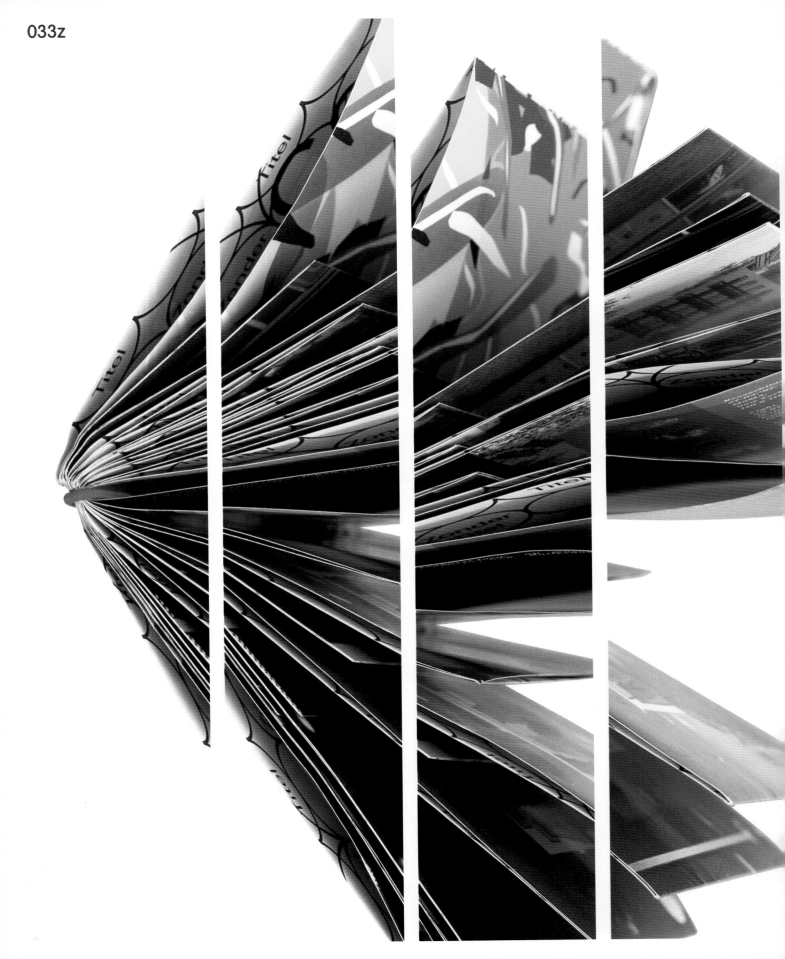

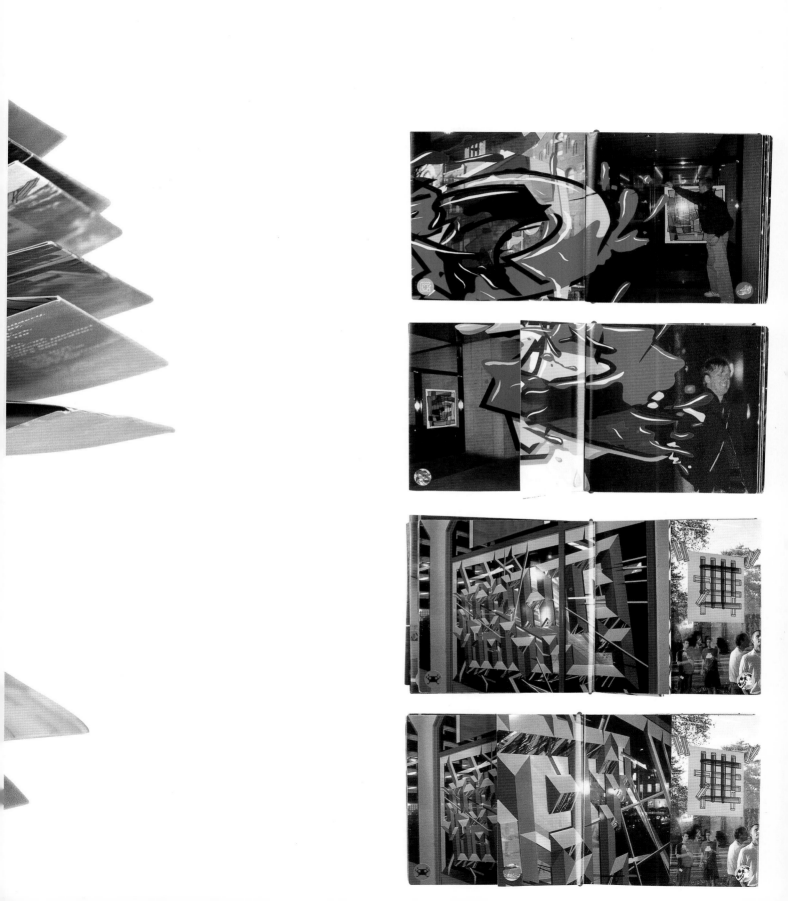

Introduction

Here is a world where the potato-headed beings run free. Where folk music is Heavy Metal and citizens are well instructed in the value of discipline. Where primitive tribes roam the ancient mountains and the little people watch from the shadows. Here is World of Pain.

Contents

序章

ここは、ジャガイモ族の自由世界。民族音楽は ヘビーメタ 市民のしつけは徹底管理。原始人が悠久の山を歩き回り、 の目が闇よりじっと見つめている。ここが、ワールド・オ ペイン、苦悩の世界へようこそ。

目次

Published by Silas & Marie Ltd
© James Jarvis · World of Pain

3

8

7

Dancing with Elves ダンシング ウィズ エルヴィス

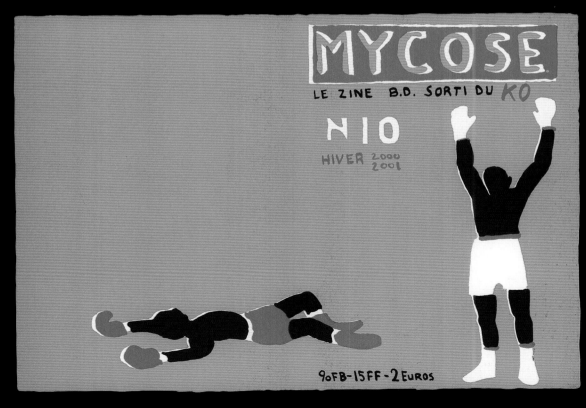

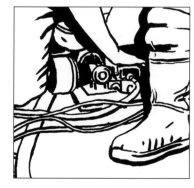

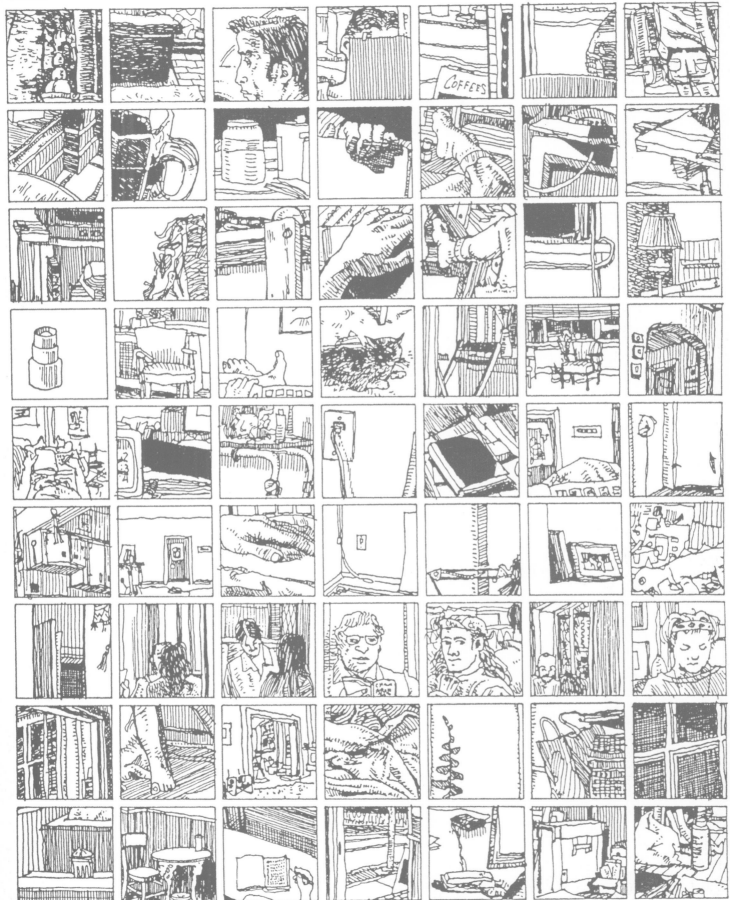

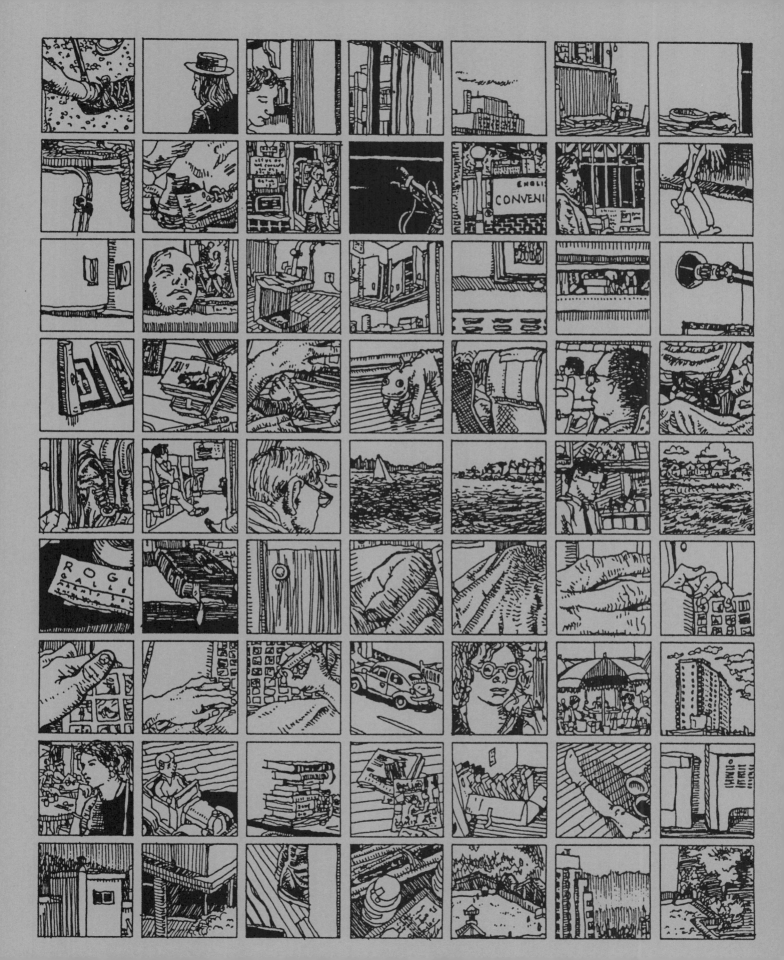

paper's paper, graph back words, memory machine, crow enuf, depending on how you fold it (box, honey-five-hundred, up on the net, rubber button, recycle minds, one times one, we arrived at todo el mundo, void and darkness, auto means self, conceal your gender, incipit not insipid, they had a little girl?, eventiality (one iota of a difference, devant-garde, taste the sun™, books as wares, on the air is into the air, I owe the, ess slash he, all's egg, by the time you get this it will be too late, relaxes with a twenty-six of, how to scat, the telegraph sender costs two or three grand, progress unmade, this is like now !?(, look for the sign for the, already continuing, schmote, seventh month old, is that black or white?, yes today,

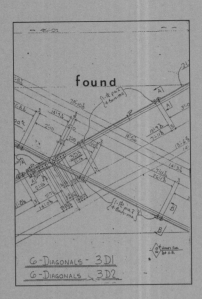

SCORCH

ERSPIRATION
STAINS

DYES AND
RUNNING COLORS

CANDY

FLYPAPER, STICKY

SCHOOL BUS

RUBBER CEMENT

SCHOOL BUS

MERCURO-CHROME

ALCOHOLIC BEVERAGES AND SOFT DRINKS

PAINTS — OIL PAINTS, VARNISHES, ENAMELS

SHOREDITCH TWAT
ISSUE 3
he's got a gun

SHOREDITCH TWAT
ISSUE 6
NICE SHADES MATE

SHOREDITCH TWAT
ISSUE 10
Two out of Ten

1st Anniversary Issue

SHOREDITCH TWAT
ISSUE 12
Not lead for your ass elf

"THE ROAD TO EXCELLENCE IS NEVER ENDING   SO THE SEARCH MUST BE UNRELENTING."

SHOREDITCH TWAT
ISSUE 2
let him have it

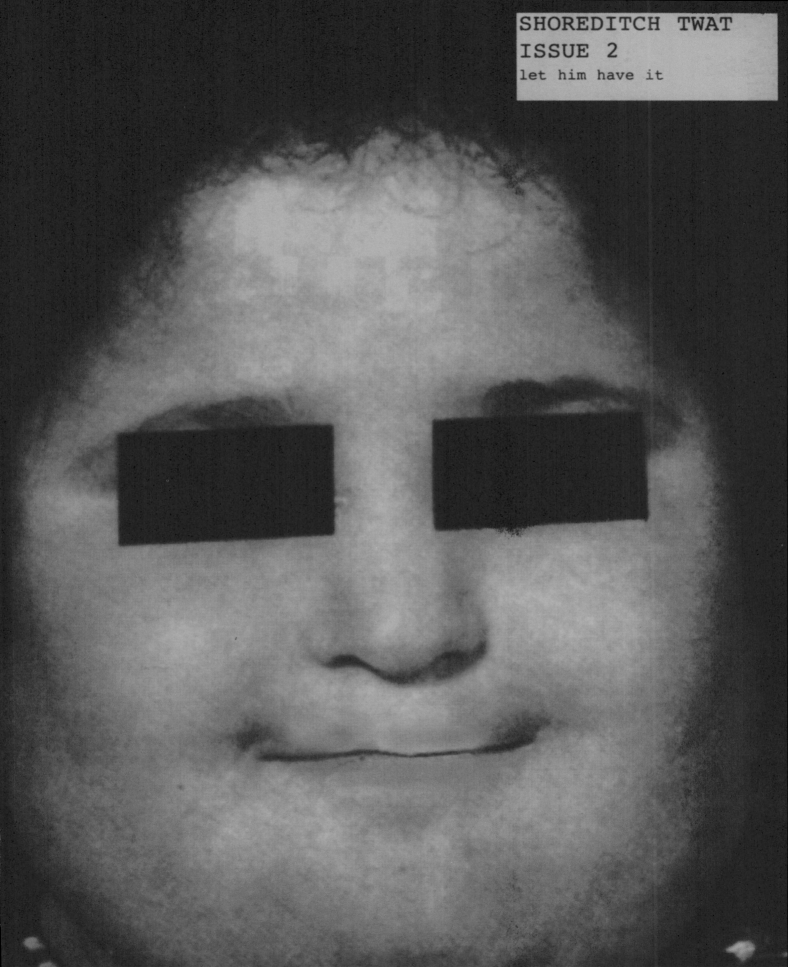

BLOW

SUPERmodel
the supermodel is dead -

long live supermodels

SUEDE
goods siezed

in midnight raid on suede

BARBIE LIVE
at thirty four

BLOW

in search of
tretchikoff

blow
goes
hello

£2.50
issue 5

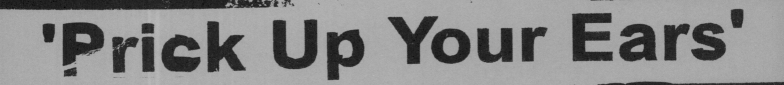
'Prick Up Your Ears'

ENJOY OUR
MAGNIFICENT
REVIEW OF
THE OUTFITS
WORN BY
IN THAILAND
IVANA TRUMP IN GLITZ AND GLAMOUR
HER PAINFUL MARRIAGE BREAK-UP
MIKE - These are photocopy duplicates if you think it'll give better results
Jacket and Pants: Red or Dead

I . MARRIED . A . CHIPPENDALE .

-WHY.DID.YOU.MARRY. A.CHIPPENDALE.

He wasn't a Chippendale when we first got married

.WHAT.WAS.HE.

An Entertainer

-.HOW.DID.YOU.FEEL.ABOUT.HIM.BECOMING.A.CHIPPENDALE.

A little bit shocked, but money is money.

SO.HE.GETS.PAID WELL.FOR.STRIPPING.THEN.-.DO.THEY .GET.PAID.BY.THE.INCH.

He doesn't strip! only sings, No they don't

WHAT.CAR.DOES.HE.DRIVE

Jeep - Automatic, with phone

IS.IT.TRUE WHAT.THEY.SAY.ABOUT.B.C.S.D.Then

its not true!!

WHAT.WOULD.YOU..SAY.TO.TO.ALL. . THOSE WOMEN

AND.NOT.A.FEW.MEN-WHO.WOULD.LIKE.TO.BE.IN.THE

POSITION.YOURE.IN

Don't do it. - marry that is .

.WHY.NOT

Mystery

$1.00

#2

ONE GAL'S
GUIDE
TO
GOOD STUFF

Date

Mystery Date #4

one dollar and fifty cents

"One Gal's
Guide to
Good Stuff"

In This Issue:
- Marriage Guides for
  the Perplexed
- Vonda Kay Van Dyke &
  the Miss American Dream
- Charm and Beauty on Vinyl
- More, More, More!

mystery date

one gal's guide to good stuff

$1.50

In this issue: Period Piece, Single Living, Records for the Feminine Lifecycle

no. five

MYSTERY

date

number six

One Gal's Guide to Good Stuff

$2.00

$1.50

Mystery Date

ONE GAL'S GUIDE TO GOOD STUFF

In This Issue:

Books About Jayne Mansfield

More Games for Girls!

Mystery Date Film Fest

#3

one dollar

Mystery Date

One Gal's Guide to Good Stuff

#1

BEFORE

AFTER

T.V. DINNER

amp
minizine

Inspirational living for modern females

Issue eight

Free!

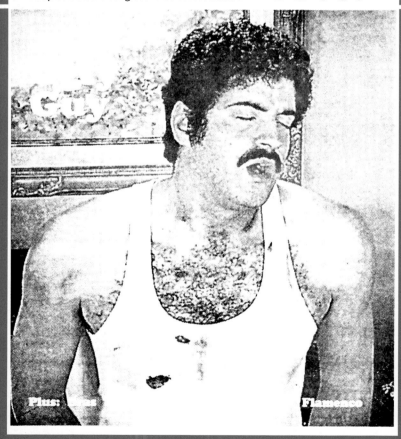

aMPMINIZINE

ISSUE 10   STYLE FOR THE CHALLENGED   FREE!

GIRLS
ROCK
OUT
ISSUE 10/10

CHEAP DATE

Joan Jett

FREE FLEXIDISC INSIDE

spring 2000

$15.00

patti

destiny

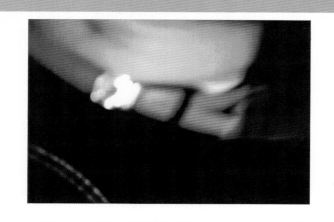

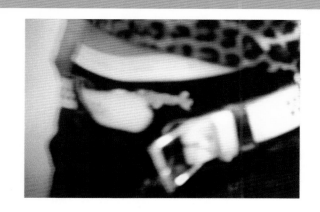

new
arrivals

(hot hot hot)

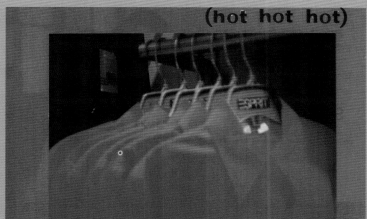

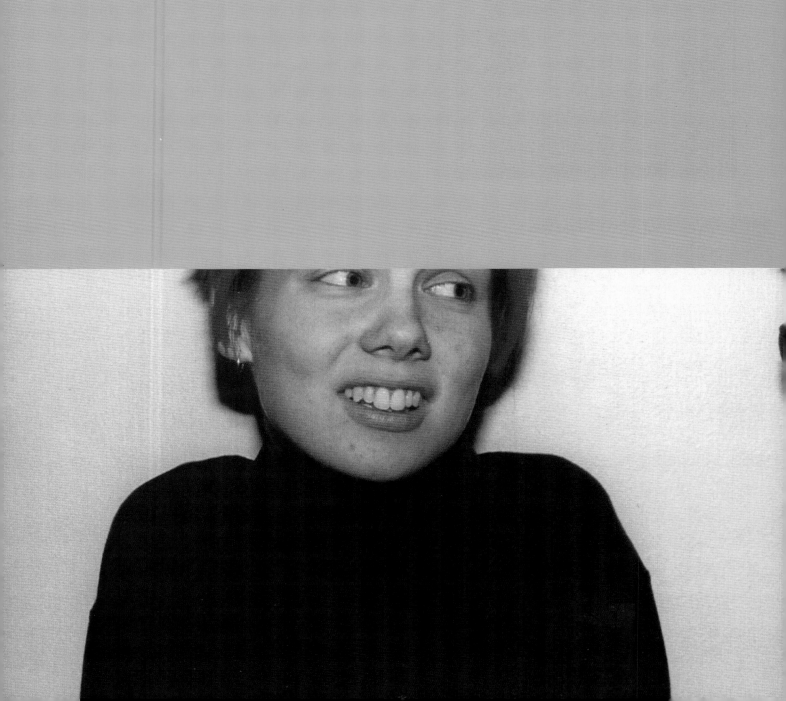

048z

SYSTEM

ACTUALLY, I TAKE THAT BACK. I DON'T NEED AN EXCUSE.

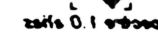

"While economic textbooks claim that people and corporations are competing for markets and resources, I claim that in reality they are competing for money -- using markets and resources to do so. So designing new money systems really amounts to redesigning the target that orients much human effort. Furthermore, I believe that greed and competition are not a result of immutable human temperament; I have come to the conclusion that greed and fear of scarcity are in fact being continuously created and amplified as a direct result of the kind of money we are using. For example, we can produce more than enough food to feed everybody, and there is definitely enough work for everybody in the world, but there is clearly not enough money to pay for it all. The scarcity is in our national currencies. In fact, the job of central banks is to create and maintain that currency scarcity. The direct consequence is that we have to fight with each other in order to survive."

--Bernard Lietaer-- http://www.ratical.org/many_worlds/cc/

A MESSAGE FROM MANAGEMENT
WILL THE LAST WORKER FIRED FROM THEIR JOB, PLEASE TURN OUT THE LIGHTS, AND TAKE OUT THE GARBAGE.

HOLIDAY IN THE SUN
a zine about surviving exposure to the mainstream

Number 2 Dollars

AVERAGE SENTE-
ENCE FOR A 1ST
TIME FEDERAL
DRUG OFFENDER: 6.9 YEA-
RS. AVERAGE SENTENCE
FOR A FIRST TIME OFFEN-
DER CONVICTED OF MANS-
LAUGHTER: 2.2 YEARS.

NUMBER OF MO-
NTHS AFTER MA-
RTIN LUTHER KI-
NG JR. PUBLICLY CALLED
THE US THE "WORLD'S
GREATEST PURVEYOR OF
VIOLENCE" THAT HE WAS
KILLED: 2

IN THE US: 1.5 MILLION
STUDENTS BROUGHT
GUNS TO SCHOOL
LAST YEAR. THE LE-
ADING CAUSE OF DEATH OF
CHILDREN AGES 1-20 YEARS
OLD IS GUNSHOT WOUNDS.
29% OF HIGH SCHOOL BOYS
HAVE A GUN.

DEATHS THRO-
UGH GUNS IN
1998: 2 IN NEW
ZEALAND, 30 IN GREAT
BRITAIN, 113 IN CANA-
DA, 213 IN JAPAN, AND
35,000 IN THE US.

AN AVERAGE
OF 34 PUBLIC
SCHOOL STU-
DENTS ARE EXPELLED
EACH SCHOOL DAY F-
OR GUN POSSESSION

NUMBER OF INSTIT-
UTIONS THAT WERE ON
"HIGHER MORAL GROU-
ND" THAN THE WORLD
BANK, ACCORDING TO THE
PRESIDENT: 0. AMOUNT THE
WORLD BANK SPEND LAST YEAR
TO GILD THE CEILINGS OF ITS
WASHINGTON HEADQUARTERS:
$400,000

NUMBER OF
TIMES THAT A
WHITE MAN HAS
BEEN EXECUTED FOR
KILLING A BLACK MAN IN
TEXAS SINCE 1860: 0

AMOUNTS THE
CALIFORNIA
PRISON SYSTEM
HAS SPENT SINCE 1993
TO PREVENT BIRDS FROM
BEING ELECTROCUTED
BY ITS FENCES: $3,400,000

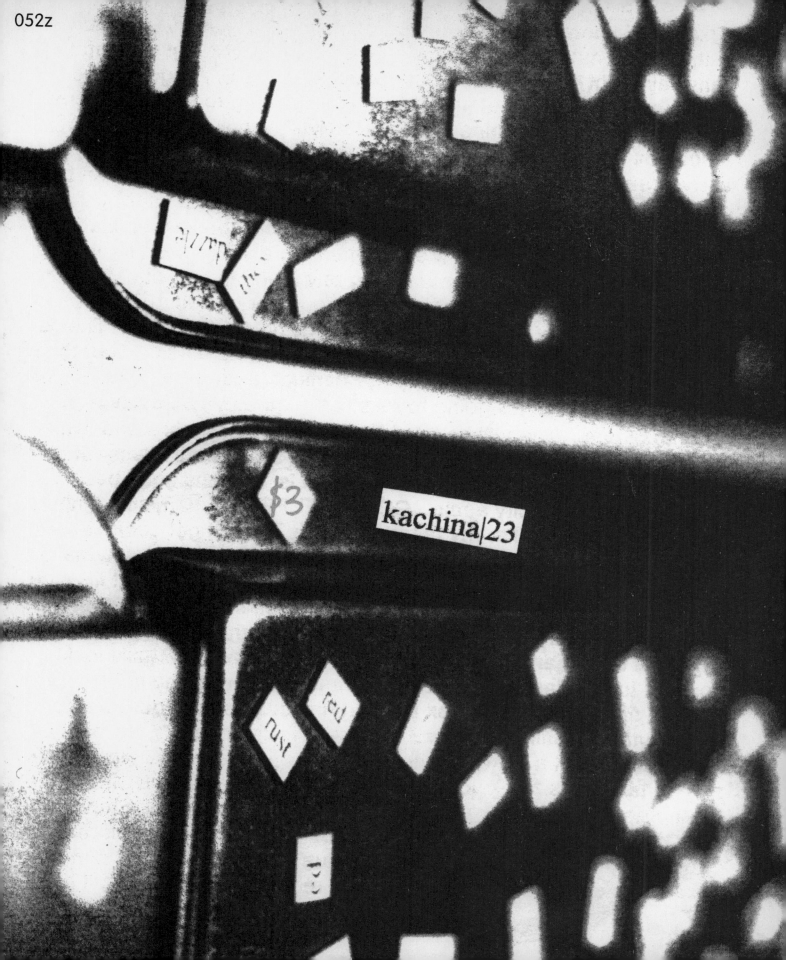

kachina|23

NO
NON
ZENZ

ELVIS
LIVES
LEVIS
EVILS

I RESENT
BREATHING
THE SHIT
FROM
YOUR CAR

TOOL
ENGINE
SHAFT
PISTON
RAMROD
WEAPON

DICKHEAD

EAT YOUR OWN SPERM

difficult
is always
thinking

i talk too much
i eat too much
i sit too much
i waste too much
i drive too much
i view too much
i moan too much
i spend too much
i fly too much
i reject too much
i burn too much
i hate too much
i believe too much
i depend too much
i consume too much
i gush too much
i evade too much
i pollute too much
i own too much
i wank too much
i snigger too much
i accept too much
i letch too much
i boast too much
i deny too much

i think too little

THEY SAID THE REVOLUTION WOULD NOT BE TELEVISED.....

the end of the beginning

Claremont Road
E11 not M11

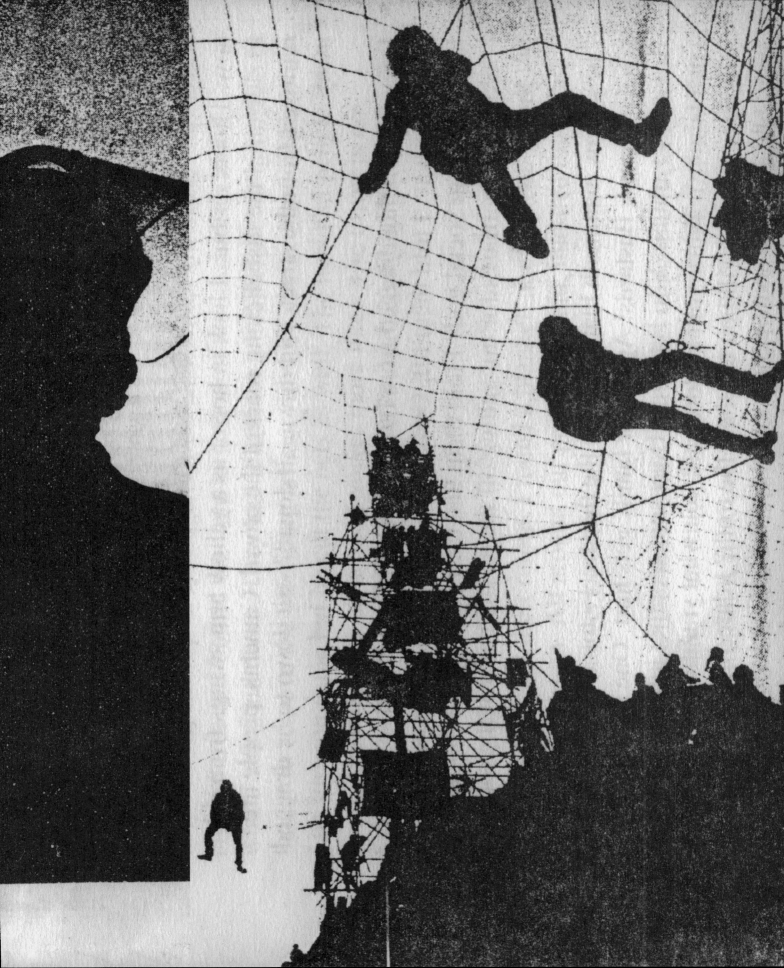

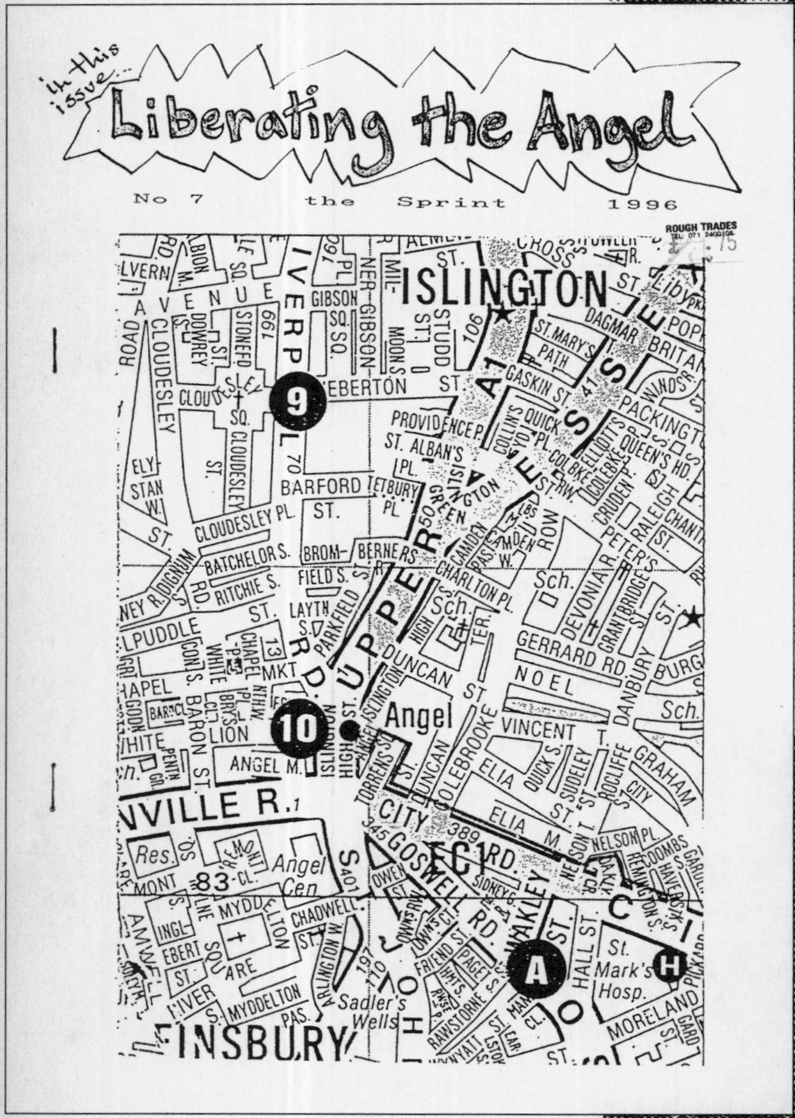

in this issue...

Liberating the Angel

No 7   the Sprint   1996

ROUGH TRADES
TEL 071 2400194
£1.75

Climb up   in s

   climb in   the h

utter needles   a

      guess   a wh

guess   is   hangir

ght

nole

d a

ole

R·W

TWO STEAKS

THE IDLEWILD FANZINE

ISSUE SIX   AUTUMN 2000

BUNKY RECORDS

vertigo #6

NATIONALLY DISTRIBUTED BY SCEPTER RECORDS INC. • 254 WEST 54th STREET, NEW YORK, NEW YORK

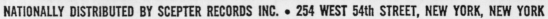

$1

HOW YA
LIKE
ME NOW
Untalented Fools
*100 ass-smacking PROOF

ENTED
LS
We Have a
Feminist
Tilt
UNTAI
FOO

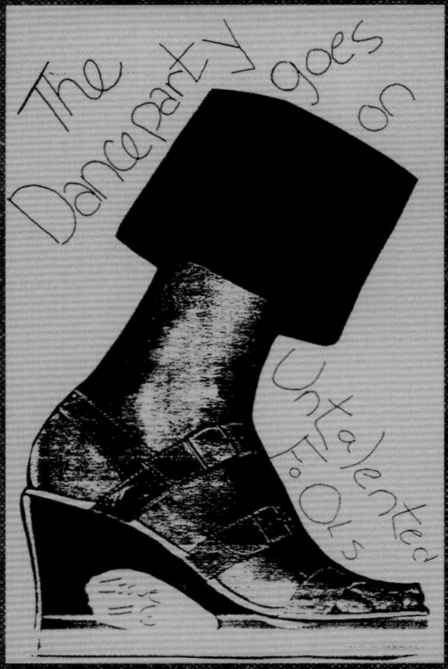

The Danceparty goes so
Untalented
FoOls

X
E
S
Untalented
F.OLS

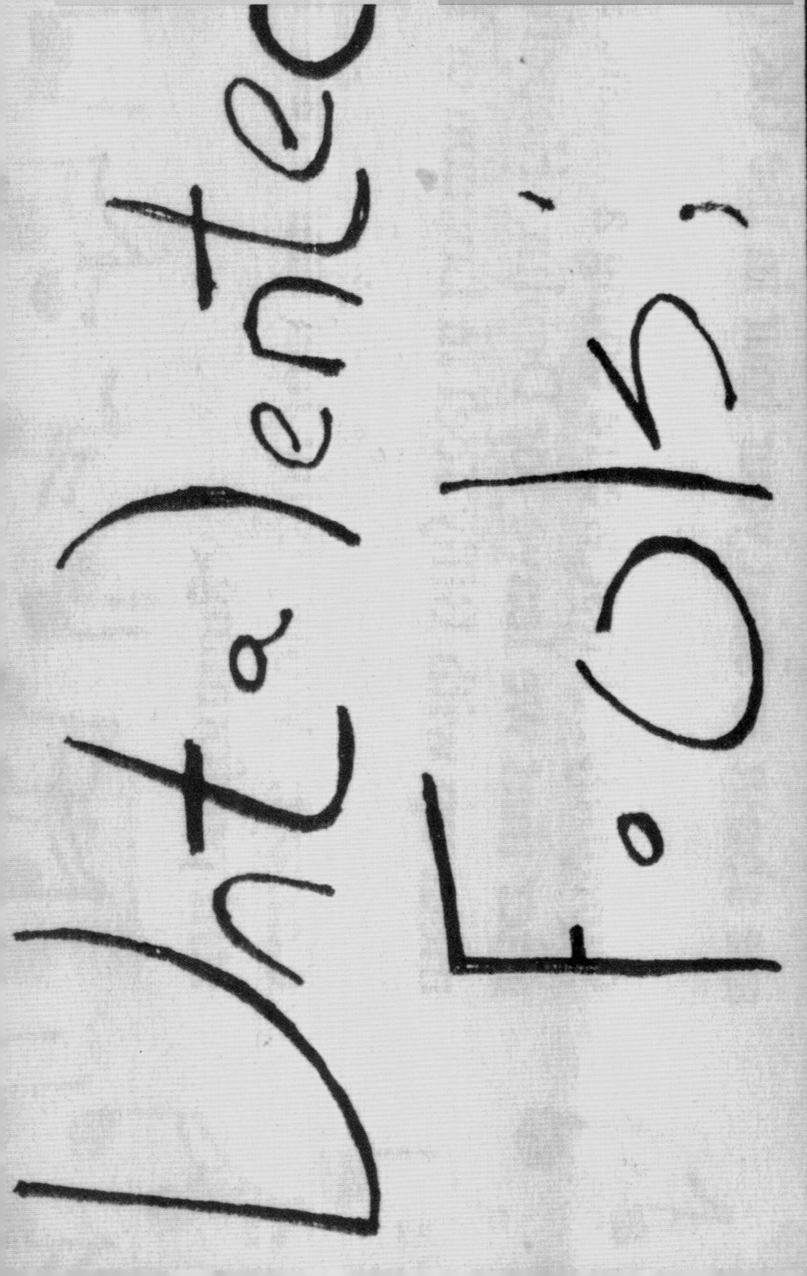

Untalented
FoOls

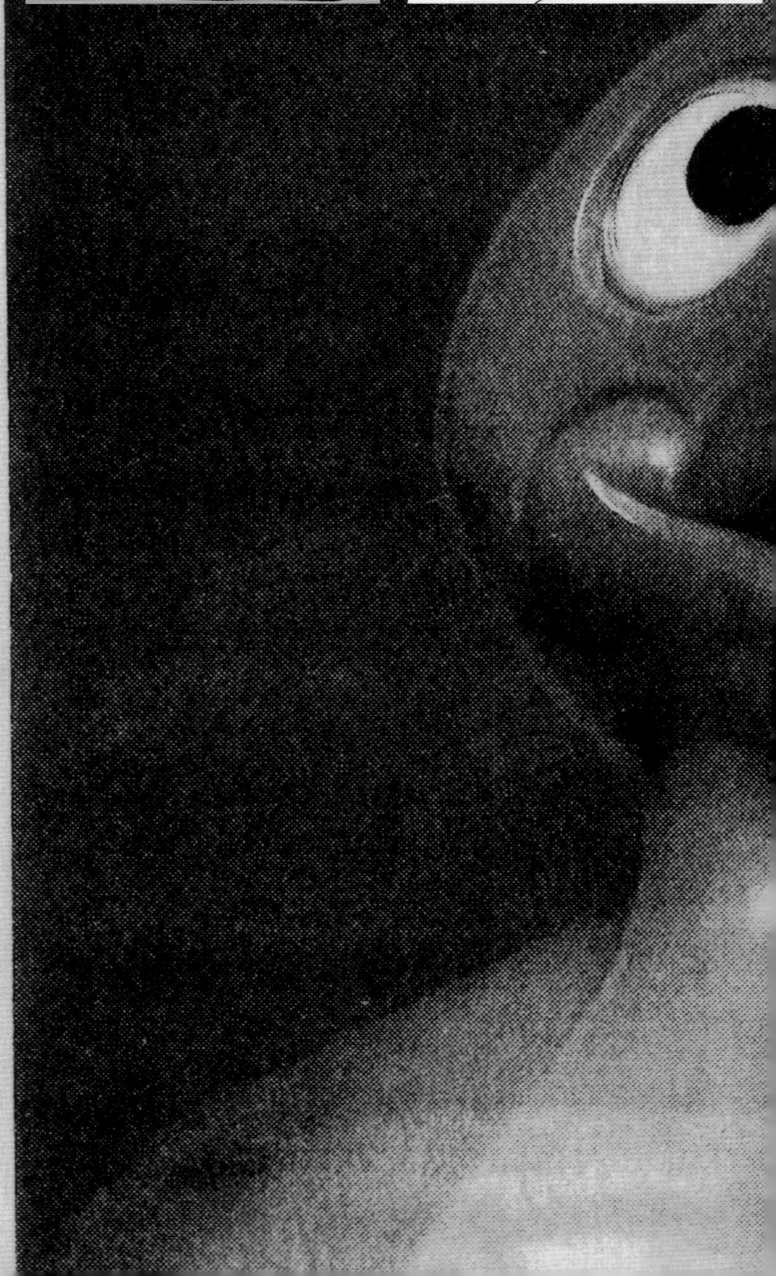

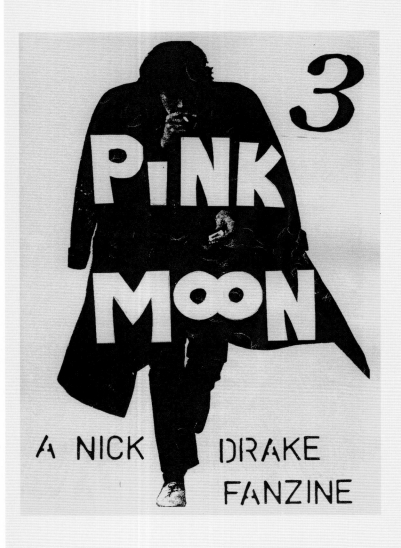

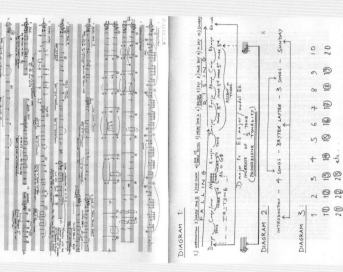

PHOTO: ISLAND RECORDS

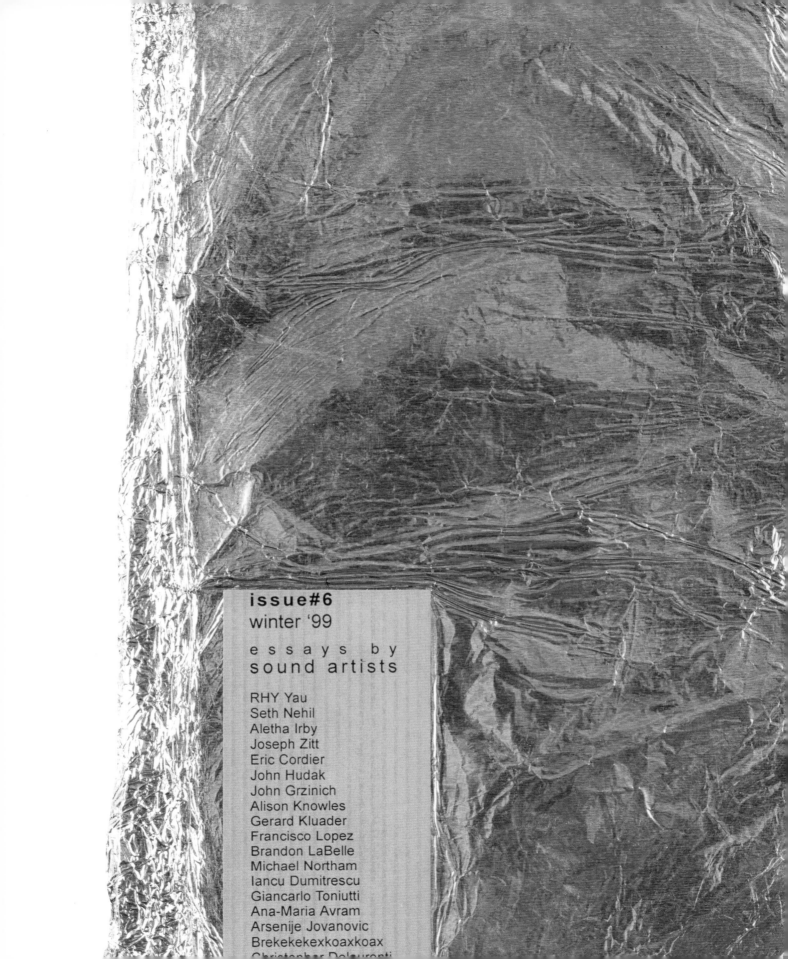

issue#6

winter '99

e s s a y s   b y
sound artists

RHY Yau
Seth Nehil
Aletha Irby
Joseph Zitt
Eric Cordier
John Hudak
John Grzinich
Alison Knowles
Gerard Kluader
Francisco Lopez
Brandon LaBelle
Michael Northam
Iancu Dumitrescu
Giancarlo Toniutti
Ana-Maria Avram
Arsenije Jovanovic
Brekekekexkoaxkoax
Christopher Delaurenti

mUsteLa fАro:

THINKER,
ARCHITECT,
FUTURIST

INTRODUCTION:

THE
CALIFORNICATE
JUXTAPOSITIONS

EXCERPTS FROM
THE **BOOK**

MUSTELIDAE
MUSTELIDAE,
WHAT ARE YOU TODAY?

MUSTELIDAE MUSTELIDAE, WHAT
ARE YOU TODAY? IS A BOOK
CONCEIVED AS A SCORE. IT IS NOT
PRECONCEIVED, AND HAS
DEVELOPED ITS OWN SHAPE
WHILE A WORK IN PROGRESS

JOIN US IN **THE STURGGLE.**

ARCHITECTURE SURVIVES IN WHAT
MICHEL FOUCAULT HAS CALLED
"HETEROTOPIAS": CAFES, RAILROAD
STATIONS, REST HOMES,
PSYCHIATRIC CLINICS, PRISONS,
CEMETERIES, THEATERS, MUSEUMS,
LIBRARIES, FAIRS. SUCH PLACES ARE
IN THEMSELVES "OTHER," FRAGMENTS
OF A UTOPIAN WORLD FLOATING IN
THE REAL WORLD, DISTORTED
MIRRORS OF REALITY WHOSE FLOOR
PLANS ARE MAPS FOR POSSIBLE
OTHER WORLDS.

THE FACT OF THE "UNPRESENTABILITY OF
THE UNPRESENT" IS AT THE VERY HEART
OF THE MODERN DILEMMA, AS THE CON-
STANT DEFERRAL OF THAT WHICH MIGHT
SATISFY US OR PRODUCE MEANING: IT IS
THE ENGINE THAT KEEPS US PRODUCTIVE
AND CONSUMPTIVE. IT IS OUR OPIUM, THAT
WHICH GIVES A PROFOUNDLY FALSE,
STERILE, AND TRAGIC CHARACTER TO
BOTH MODERN SOCIETY AND ITS REPRE-
SENTATION IN CULTURAL ARTIFACTS.
THOSE ARTIFACTS CAN ONLY CONFRONT
US WITH A LACK OF MEANING, OR ITS
PRESENCE IN THE ABSOLUTE OF DEATH.
THEY CAN MAKE US AWARE OF THE LACK
OF ORDER, OF THE FAILURE OF THE AMERI-
CAN DREAM AND ITS ARCHITECTURE.
THEY CAN SHOW US THE MIASMA OF OUR
URBAN ENVIRONMENT, IN WHICH IT IS IN-
CREASINGLY DIFFICULT TO DISTINGUISH
BETWEEN THE IMAGE OF MAN, OR MA-
CHINE, OR MAN/MACHINE ACCORDING TO
WHICH WE LIVE. WITH THE CREATION OF
MASS MEDIA, ARCHITECTURE CANNOT
RECREATE US; IT CAN ONLY MAKE US
AWARE OF OUR ABSENCE OF SELF. IT
MUST ALLOW US TO LIVE IN A WORLD OF
APPEARANCES, IN OTHER WORDS, IN A
WORLD MADE BY MAN, THE SCENE ON
WHICH HE APPEARS AND WHICH MAKES
HIM A MEMBER OF HUMANITY, AND MUST
MAKE THAT WORLD PART OF US.

$3

loud paper

dedicated to increasing the volume of architectural discourse

The 1992 BMW driveaway car on the scenic overlook in Lewiston, Idaho looking at Clarkston, Washington, 4-24-99

volume 3, issue 2

WE MUST BEGIN BY UNDERSTANDING ARCHITECTURE AS A CRITICAL INVESTIGATION AND AS AN ACT OF PERCEPTION THAT WILL ALLOW US TO REMAKE A COMMUNITY IN WHICH WE CAN MIRROR OUR HUMANITY - A TRUE UNITY: THE REMAKING OF THE MATERIAL OF EXPERIENCE IN THE ACT OF EXPRESSION ... IS ALSO A REMAKING OF THE EXPERIENCE OF COMMUNITY IN THE DIRECTION OF GREATER ORDER AND COMMUNITY. AT THE SAME TIME, WE MUST REALIZE THAT, AS WE STILL LIVE UNDER THE SIGN OF MODERNIZATION, THIS WILL BE A MODERN PROJECT, OR RATHER THE PROJECT OF THE MODERN: THE PROJECTION OF OURSELVES INTO THE WORLD PERCEIVED AS TECHNOLOGICALLY FRAGMENTED, INIMICAL, VIOLENT AND ESSENTIALLY DESTRUCTIVE TO OUR HUMANITY.

"THE POSTMODERN WOULD BE THAT WHICH, IN THE MODERN, PUTS FORWARD THE UNPRESENTABLE IN PRESENTATION ITSELF; THAT WHICH DENIES ITSELF THE SOLACE OF GOOD FORMS. ... LET US WAGE WAR ON TOTALITY; LET US BE WITNESSES TO THE UNPRESENTABLE IN PRESENTATION ITSELF; THAT WHICH DENIES ITSELF THE SOLACE OF GOOD FORMS. ... LET US WAGE WAR ON TOTALITY; LET US BE WITNESSES TO THE UNPRESENTABLE; LET US ACTIVATE THE DIFFERENCE AND SAVE THE HONOR OF THE NAME." WE MUST BEGIN TO REALIZE OURSELVES AS SATIRIC MACHINES. IN THE PAST A POSSIBILITY EXISTED FOR A CRITICAL ALTERNATIVE TO THE URBAN SCENE - THE BUCOLIC OR SATIRIC LANDSCAPE POPULATED BY THE HALF-MEN AND HALF-MONSTERS WHOSE DUBIOUS HUMANITY REBELLED AGAINST HUMAN CULTURE. OUR LANDSCAPE IS ONE OF TECHNOLOGY; ITS SATYRS ARE ROBOTS.

WE MUST LEARN TO INHABIT THIS **SCENE.** A GROWING NUMBER OF YOUNG DESIGNERS ARE MOVING INTO THE REALM OF THE MODERN WORLD. THEY ARE INVESTIGATING THE POSSIBILITY OF AN ARCHITECTURE OF **EMPOWERMENT,** AN APPROPRIATION OF TECHNOLOGY. THIS ARCHITECTURE WILL BE A CRITICAL ARTIFACTING ALLOWING US TO BREAK OPEN THE ABSENT WORLD AND PLACE US IN A MAPPED AND MIRRORED CONSTRUCTION WE IDENTIFY AS OUR **WORLD.** THEIR CONSTRUCTIONS CANNOT BE PURE HETEROTOPIAS, BECAUSE SUCH PLACES CANNOT BE STABLE OBJECTS. INSTEAD, THESE DESIGNERS **PLOT** STRATEGIES, DECONSTRUCT REALITIES, AND MAKE.

LOVE IS A SCRIPT
WITH WHICH I SAY GOODBYE

TO ARCHITECTURE AND YOU

MUSTELIDAE MUSTELIDAE,
WHAT ARE YOU TODAY?
...CALI**FORNI**CAT^E...

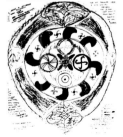

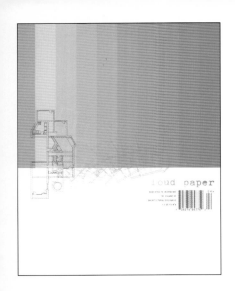

loud paper

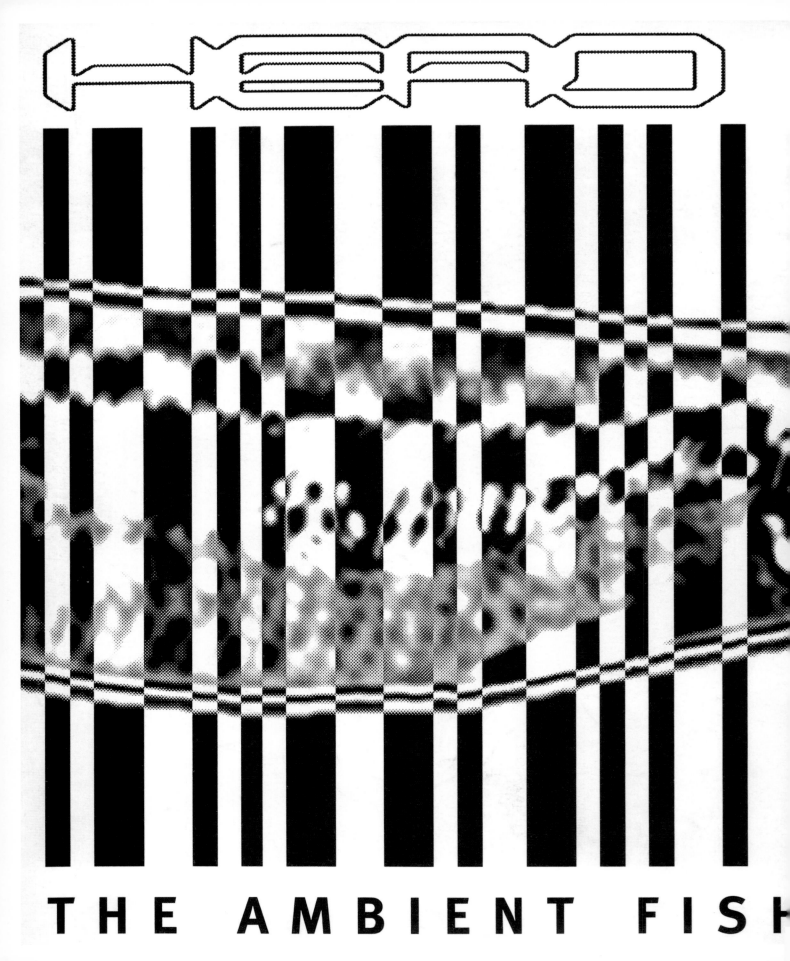

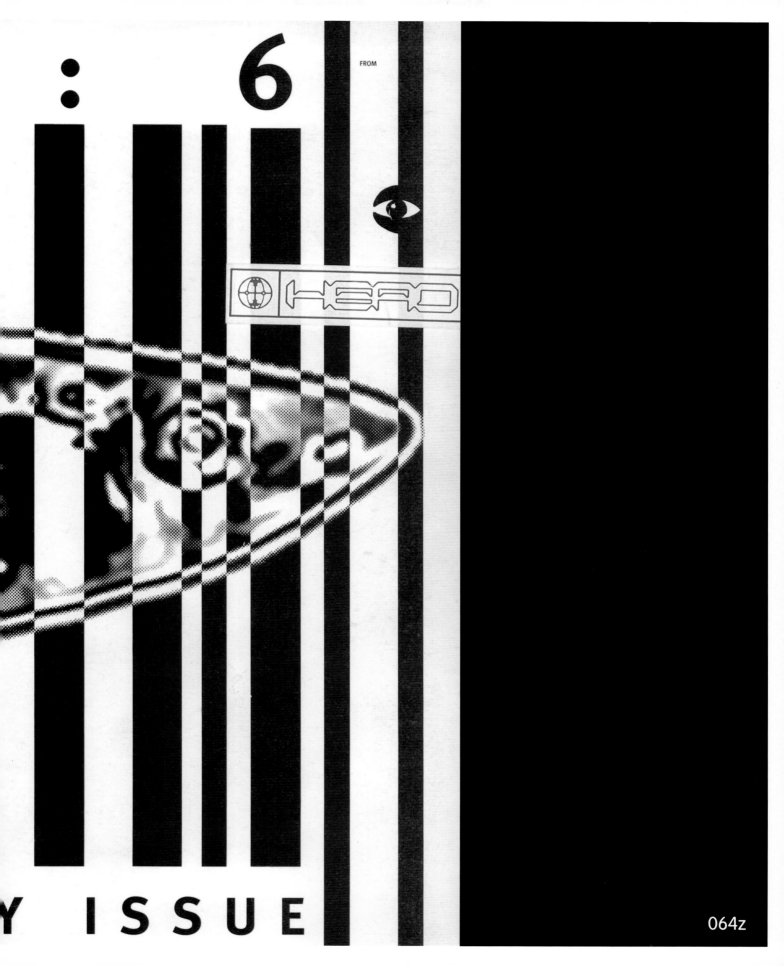

: 6 FROM

HEAD

Y ISSUE

064z

THE GRUESOME ACTS
OF CAPITALISM

Size of the Canadian government's loan to China for the purpose of buying Candu nuclear reactors:

$1.5 billion

Amount of money western countries recently used to rescue Wall Street:

$3.5 billion

Amount of money the West used to help Central Americans in the wake of Hurricane Mitch:

$300 million

Amount of money Japan gave to the military dictatorship governing Burma:

$48.7 million

Western businessmen are considering Burma as a new source of cheap labor, undercutting China and Vietnam.

Percentage of foreign aid by western countries has dropped to the lowest on record:

0.25

(The United Nations target level is 0.7)

Percentage of the world's greenhouse gasses produced by the U.S.A.:

20

Percentage of the world's population in the U.S.A.:

5

Percentage consumption of the world's resources by the U.S.A.:

33

Number of people who work in the United Nations system:

53,589

Number of people who work for Disney:

53,600

Number of people who work for McDonald's:

150,000

Number of billionaires whose net wealth is 1.5 times greater than the combined national incomes of the world's 48 least developed countries:

10

The rich get richer, the poor still get poorer…

•

Es Konnte auch anders sein. It could just as well be otherwise.

Places on planet Earth currently without McDonald's hamburgers:

Mongolia, Bermuda, Seychelles, Ecuador, Uzbekistan

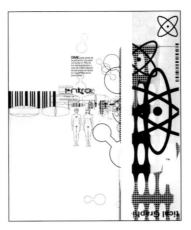

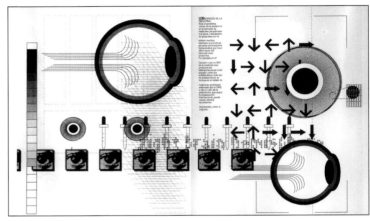

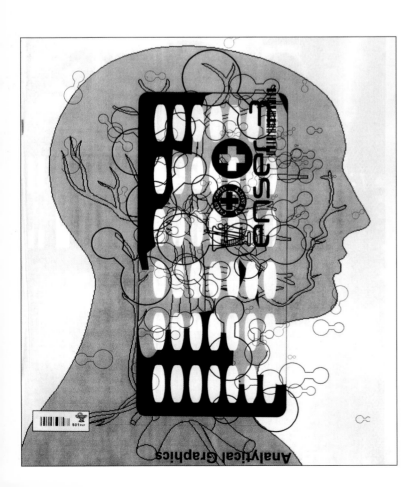

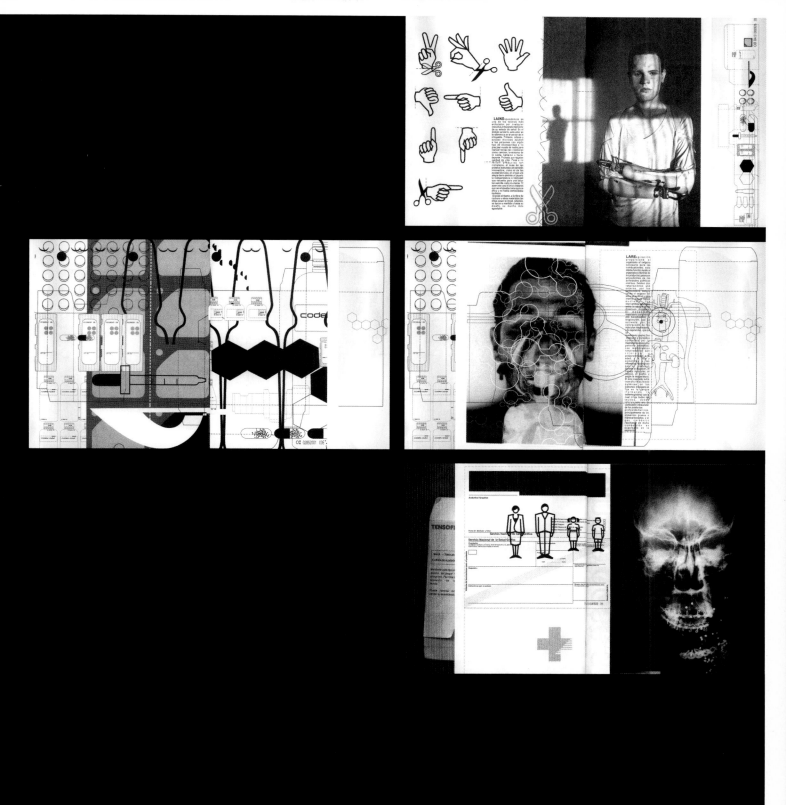

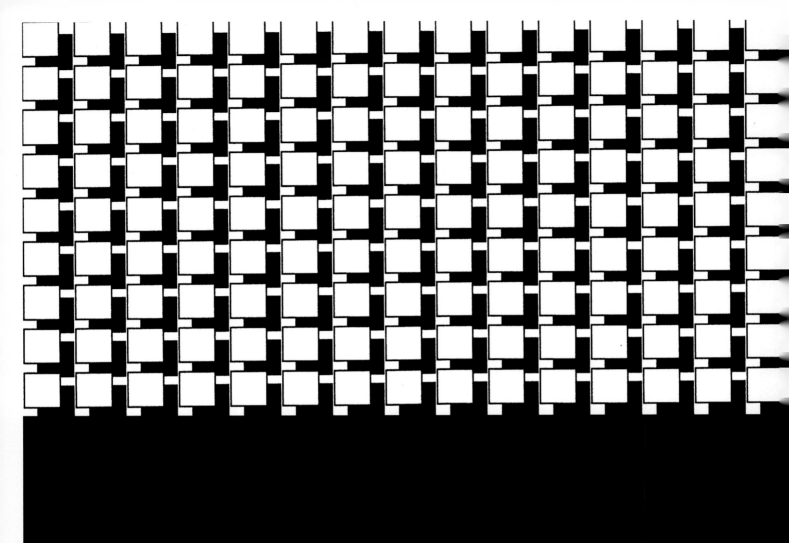

fecha/date:...
N° Pág.(Incluida ésta)Nr. Of Pages (Including cover sheet):.........................
Para/ To:..N° Tel./Phone Nr..........................
Empresa/ Company:...............................N° Fax/ Fax Nr.:......................
De/From:
Copia para/ Copy for:

FAX

€

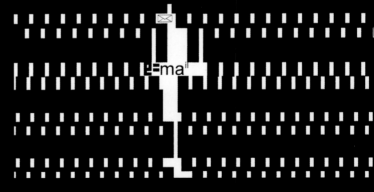

e=mail

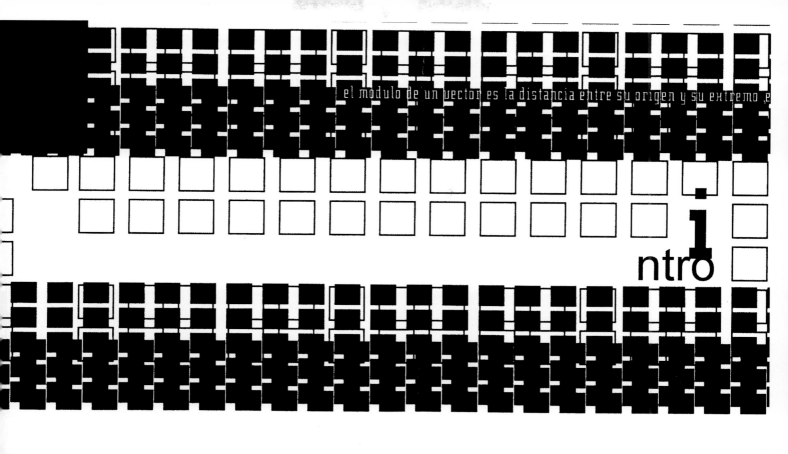

el modulo de un vector es la distancia entre su origen y su extremo e

i
ntro

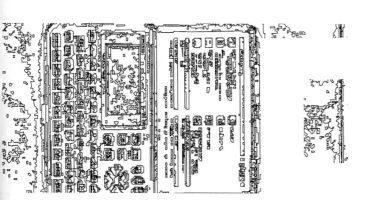

068z

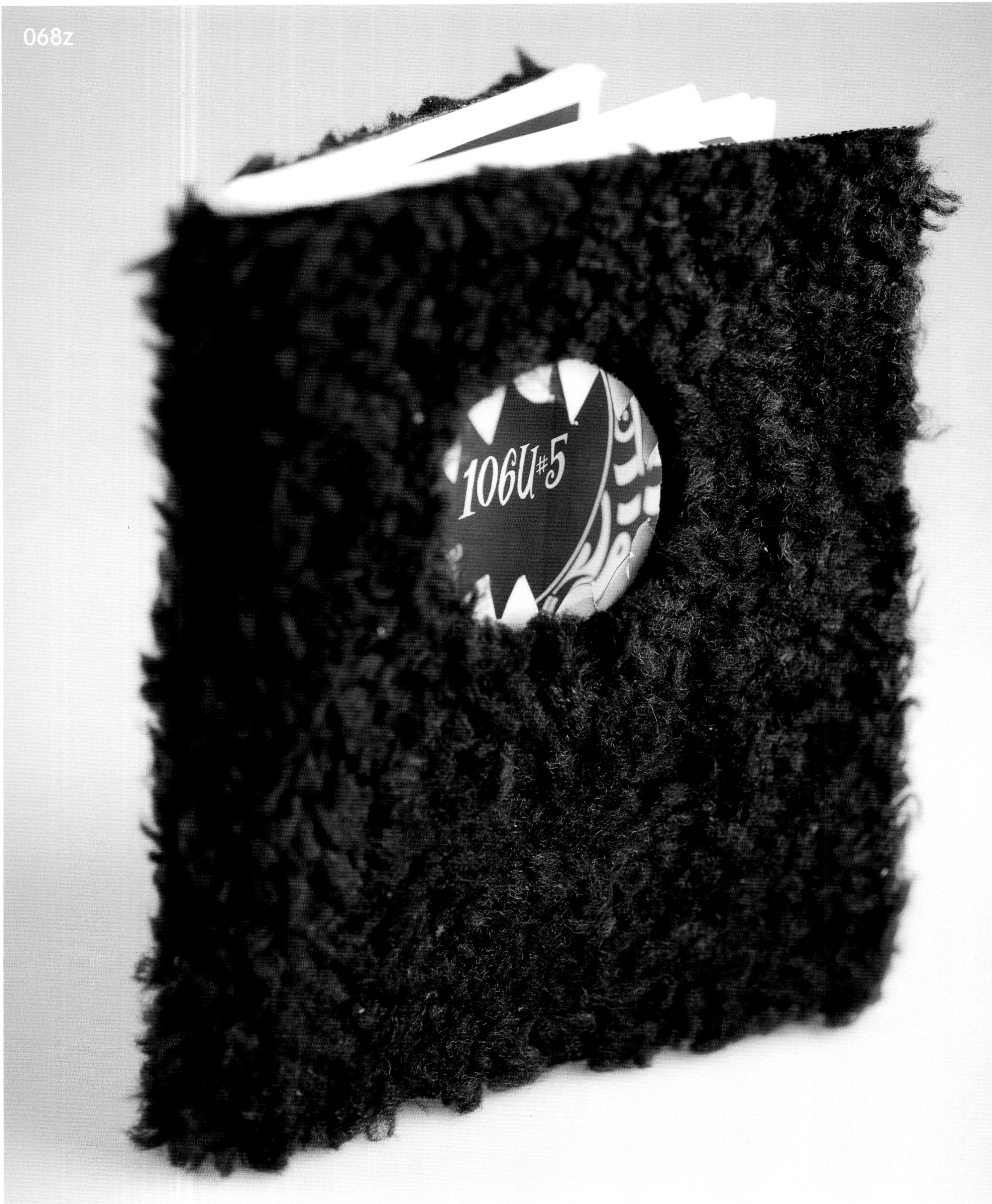

S[A]E

AUSTRALIAN MADE

~~$74·00~~

$46·00
SPECIAL

PLUS SALES TAX 11%

DANGER

OUT OF ORDER

This tag is placed _____ of an unsafe
condition and n_____ removed
except by the pe_____ attached it
and after repair_____.

DO NOT THRO
DO NOT SHIFT
DO NOT STAR
DO NOT USE THIS _____ R PIECE
OF EQUIPMENT

Tag placed by _____

Date _____ 19 _____ Time _____ p.m.

REPAIRMEN MUST SEE THAT POWER AS BEEN
DISCONNECTED BEFORE PROC _____ NG
SEE OTHER SID

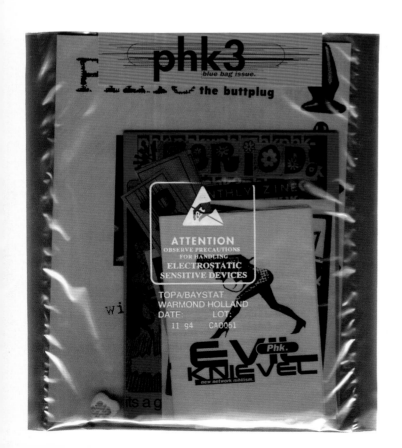

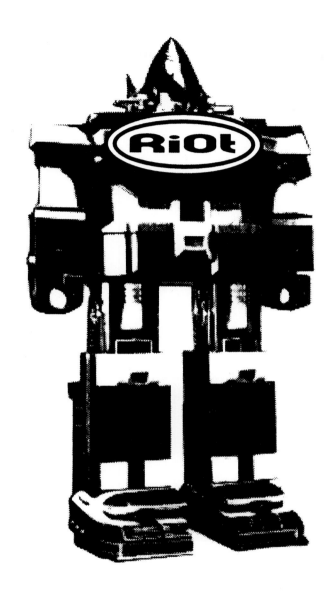

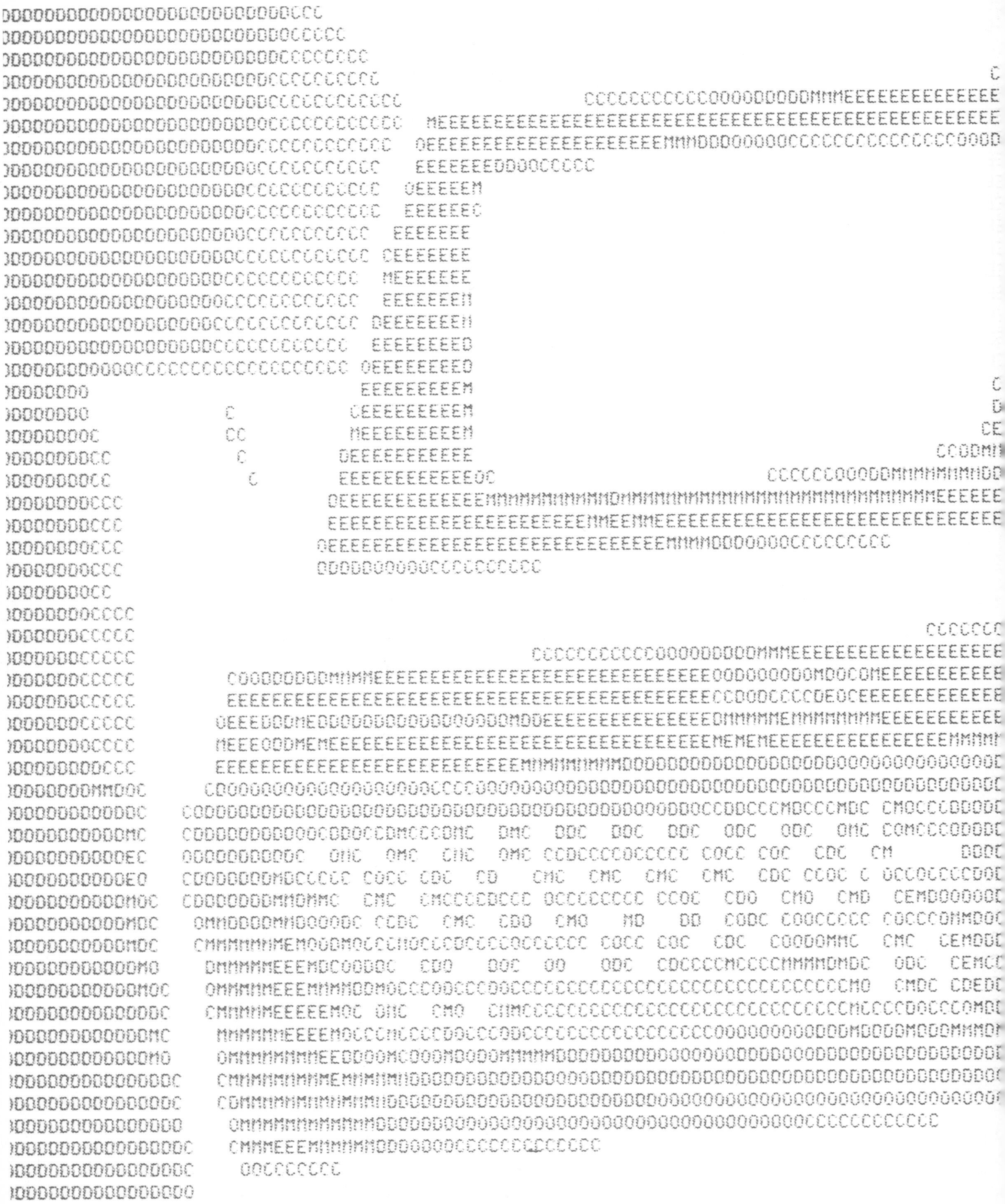

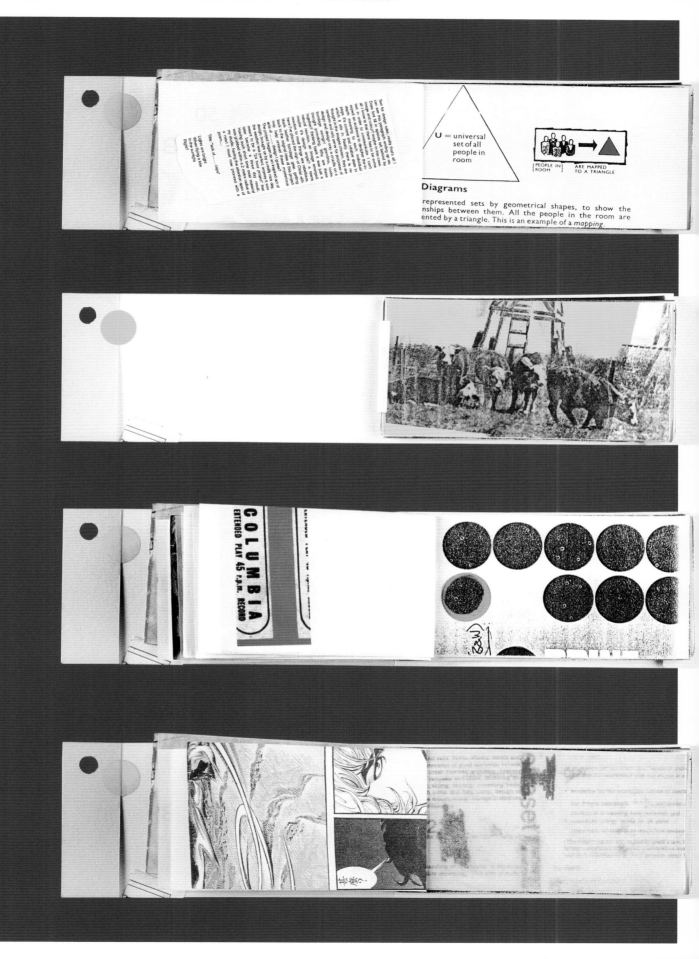

Stück

including: one 45rpm record (if you're fast and lucky!), one butchers hook, one family game, two languages, three different kinds of paper, four colours, five... many holes, and lots more!

DM **22.00** (£12)

limited edition 1189/1500

FLEISCH meat / flesh

Heft / issue no. 1, PM '94

Shift.

Achtung Sichtfenster bei Betrieb trefft!

£12

22 DM

Heft / issue	2
Thema / theme	°C
Hitze / heat	
limited edition	
	/1500

Shift:

Achtung! Original von Wee Flowers beiliegend!

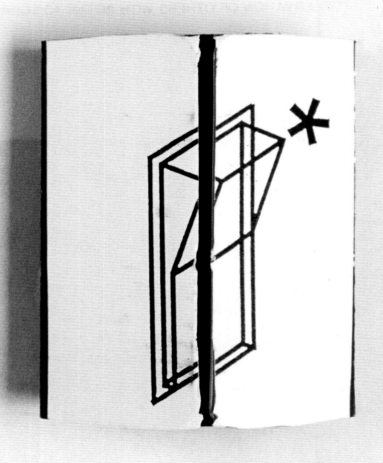

077z

the switch

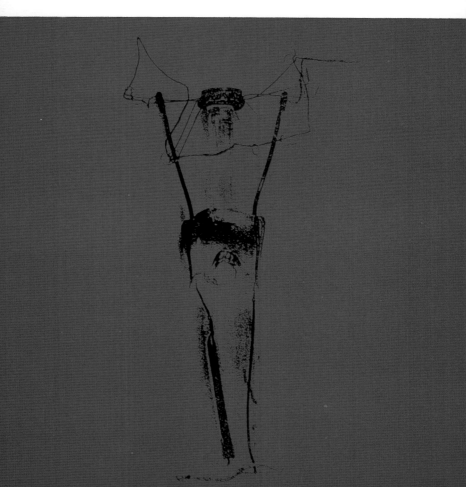

the

wiTch

Charles came in without waking them. It was the last time. He was going to say goodbye to her.

The aromatic herbs were still smoking, and the swirling blue vapours blended into the mist that was coming in through the window. There were a few stars, and the night air was mild.

The wax from the candles was falling in great drops on to the bedclothes. Charles looked at them, until his eyes were aching from the brightness of their yellow flame.

Ripples were washing over the satin dress, as pale as moonlight. Emma was disappearing into its whiteness; and to him it was just as if, flowing out of herself, she were passing darkly into the things around her, into the silence, into the night, into the passing breeze and the damp smell rising from the earth.

He had a sudden vision of her in the garden at Tostes, on the bench, by the thorn-hedge, or else on the streets of Rouen, at the door of their house, in the yard at Les Bertaux. He could still hear the laughter of the little boys dancing for joy beneath the apple-trees; the room was full of the perfume of her hair, and her dress was rippling in his arms with a crackle of sparks. The same dress, it was, the one she had on now!

He spent a long time like this, remembering his lost happiness, her movements, her gestures, the sound of her voice. After every misery, there came another, and yet another, relentlessly, like the waves of a flood-tide.

He felt a terrible curiosity: slowly, with fingertips, his heart trembling, he lifted her veil. But he gave out a cry of horror that woke the other two men. They hauled him downstairs, to the parlour.

Félicité came to say that he wanted some of her hair.

— Cut some off! said the apothecary.

She didn't dare, and so, he stepped forward himself, with the scissors in his hand. He was trembling so violently that he stabbed several little holes in the skin around her temples. In the end, steeling himself to do it, Homais chopped two or three times at random, leaving patches of white in that beautiful black hair.

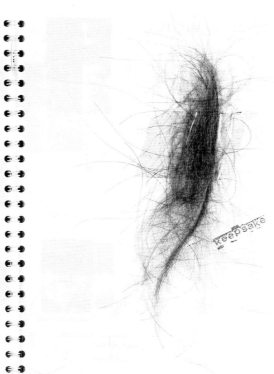

A hairy ring for
you to finger...

TOOT

ISSUE #1 *SEX*

Ring Sally
9417 2646

Jade Walsh
re: TOOT
issue #1
left 5 copies
@ $5 nett.

BEAT OUR HOT EREC...

CRAVE OUR THROB THEM

ASS COME GIG

THRUST EAT ORGAN SPREAD

The Manager
Gourmet Powder Company
180 High Street
Springvale VIC

Dear Sir,

██

███████████████████████████████████████

███████████████████████████████████████

███████████████████████████████████████

███████████████████████████████████████

███████████████████████████████████████

█████████████████████████████ tits ████████

███████████████████████████████████████

███████████████████████████████████████

████████████████████████████

Yours faithfully

B. Papps

Herbert B. Papps (Esq.)

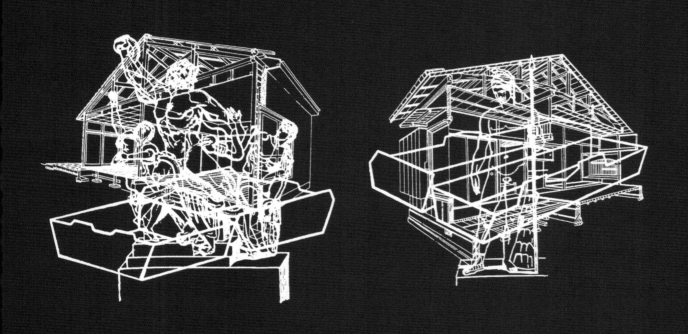

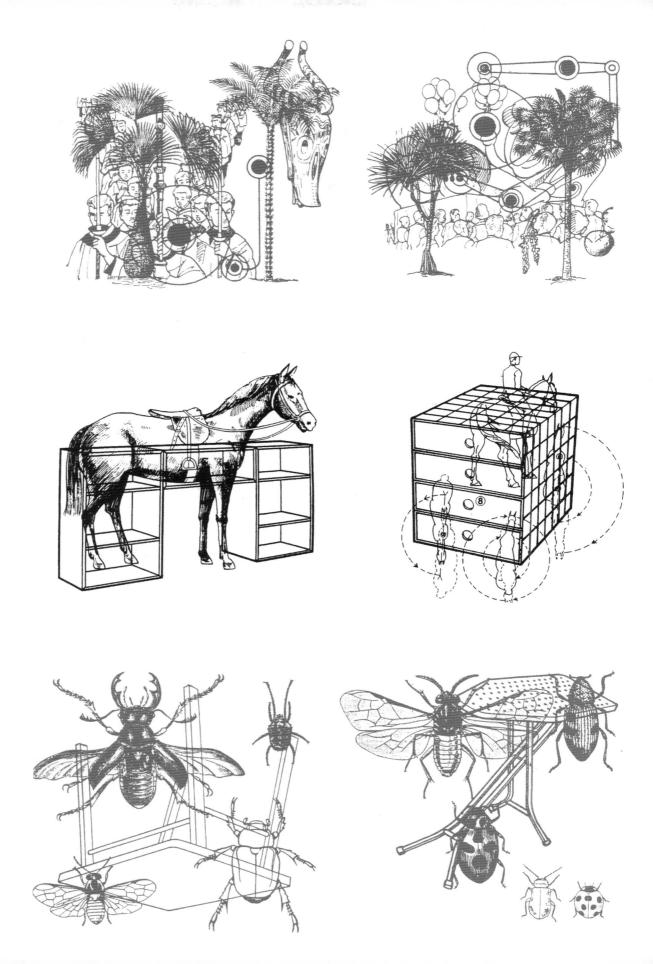

SCISSORS

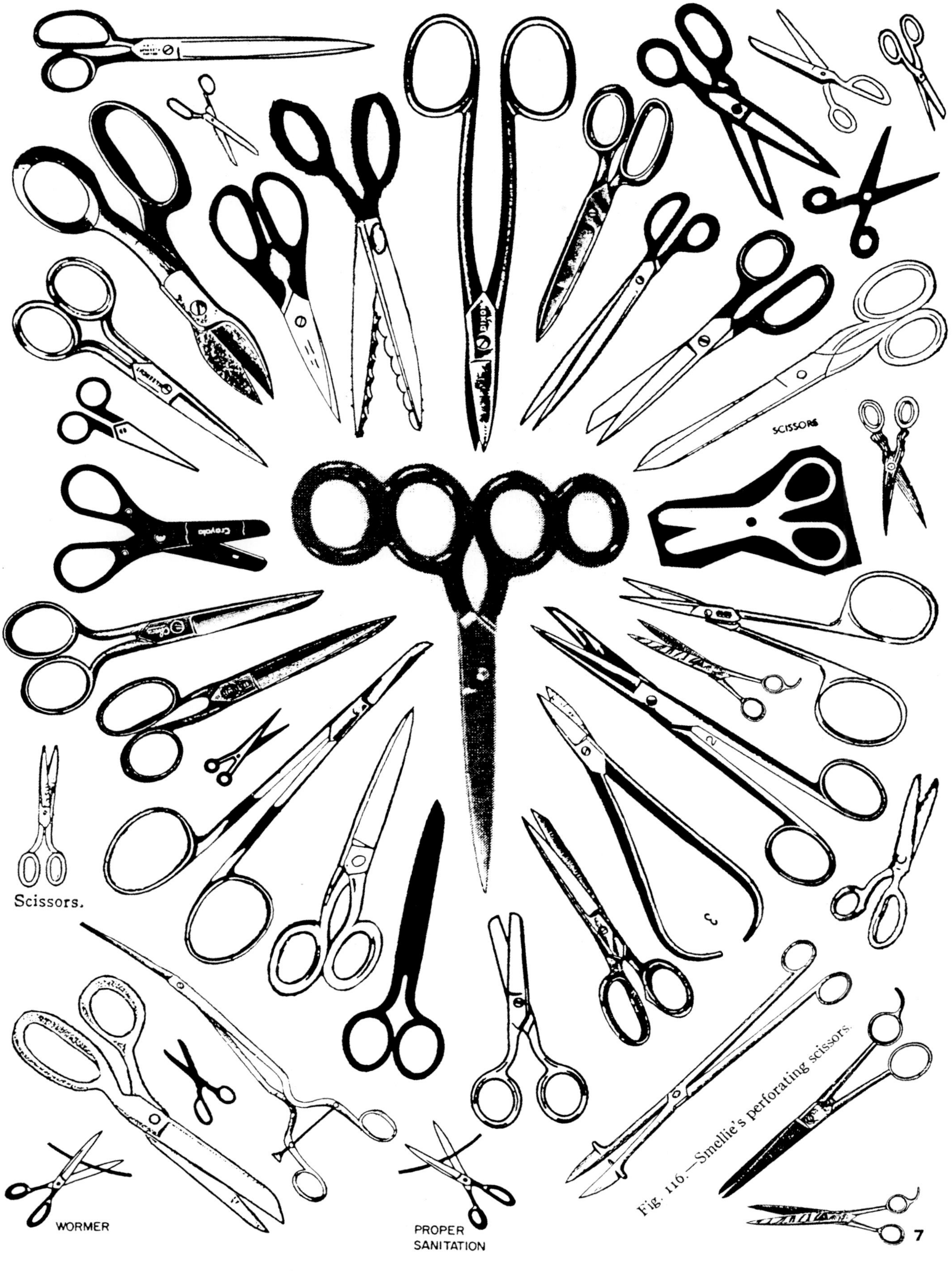

Scissors.

WORMER

PROPER
SANITATION

Fig. 116.—Smellie's perforating scissors.

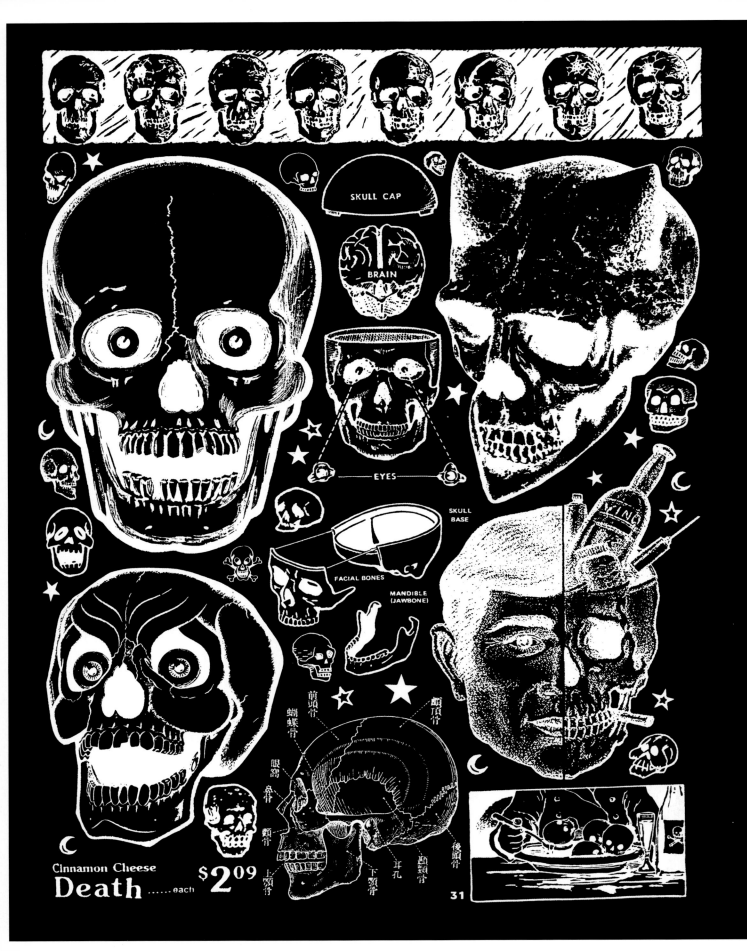

Cinnamon Cheese
Death ......each 2^{09}

31

65

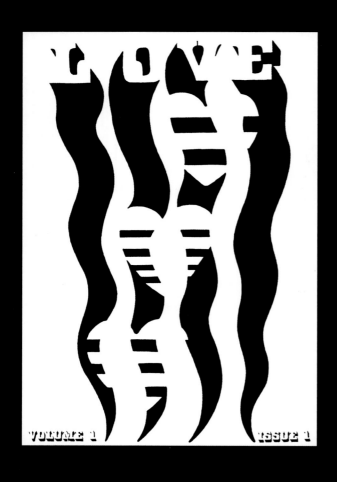

083z

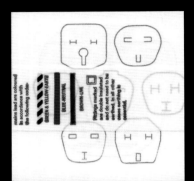

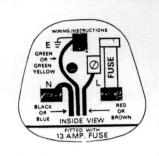

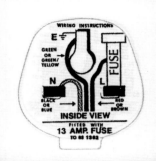

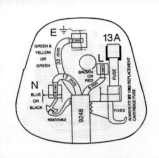

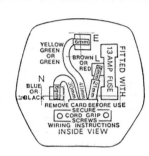

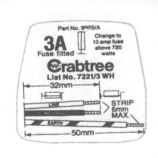

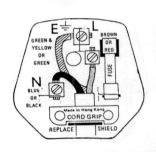

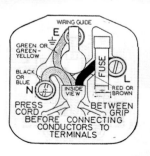

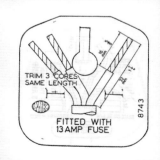

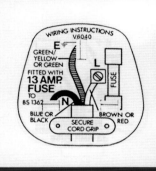

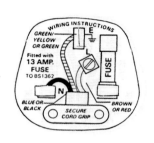

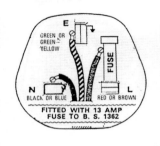

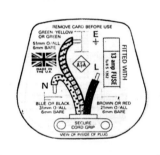

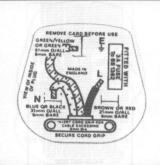

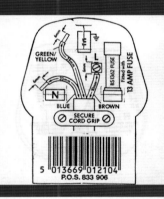

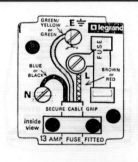

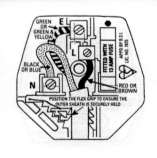

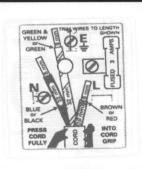

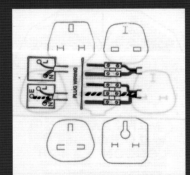

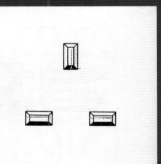

Cannibals of North America

by juliette torrez
illustrated by scott mills

SPOKANE

limping to spokane in second gear
missing some teeth
can't go any faster
than 25 miles per hour
white light and holy water
can't undo the evil done
another in a long line of bad carma
wreaking havoc on electrical systems
graduated to another kind of car trauma
gears and transmissions
days later still stuck in spokane
waiting for parts from other lands
make a list of things to sell
things to take
survival in action my reaction
sit and cry i can't it's a
kamikaze mission

OLYMPIA

headachy from cigarettes
try to recapture the day's events
left the house for a cup of latte
ended up at an all day party
sitting on the porch
bumming a smoke
reading the rag
suddenly this guy next to me asks,
"what is that bone?"
fox jaw always good for conversation
small talk about my trip my transmission
"hey," he says, "i know where
there's a really good band playing."
past deschutes past little rock
wrong turn at the driving range
past the abandoned store
up the road two miles
rainbow valley traveler's haven
you know you're there when you see
people picking strawberries
and hear the band playing

water began pouring in the house
we tied ourselves
to the kitchen counter
while hell was breaking loose
dishes flying into space
frying pan hit me in the head
almost knocking me cold
alive with fright
adrenaline rush
hold the rope tight
while ocean water
swirled around our waists
suddenly everything was still
deafening quiet
eye of the storm
nothing quite like it
over too quick
tempest in a teacup
all the water made it hard to breathe
much less scream
and looking down
i saw fish swimming
on the kitchen floor

PANHANDLE LANDSCAPE

panhandle landscape
flatter than a pancake
knocking off mile by mile
speeding through amarillo
late night coffee and cigarettes
get weird looks from interstate truckers
fat motherfuckers
picking their teeth in the corner
road trip fantasy
now i see the stupidity
plans to dance in deep ellum
maybe a tattoo at tigger's
i figured to make it right to remember

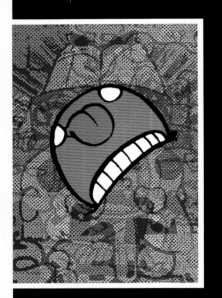

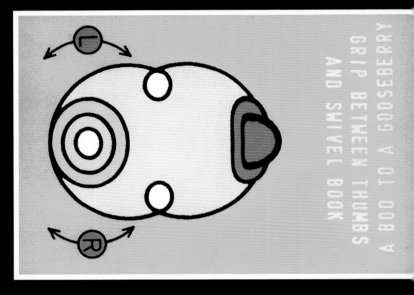

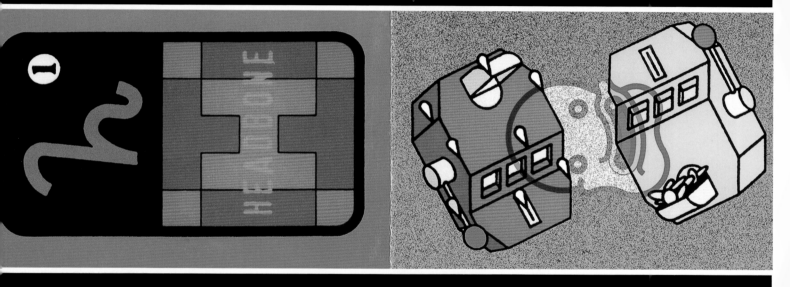

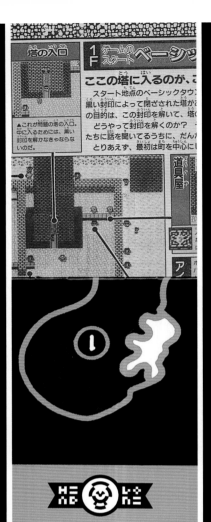

088z

Roy Lichtenstein

MATCHBOOK ART

Yoh Koshiwabaa

LAWRENCE ALLOWAY

Abbeville Modern Masters

Chronicle Books

BRUCE LEE
The Untold Story

Bruce Lee's Life
Story as Told by
the
Family and
Friends

Fully Illustrated
with Exclusive Photos
from the
Family Album

A Collector's Issue!

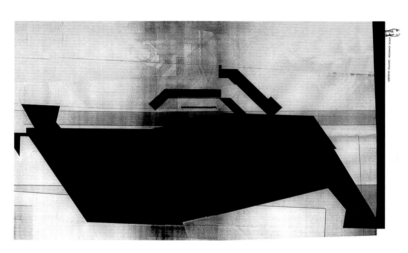

And another list...of books to read if you want more...

Duncombe, Stephen: Notes from underground, zines and the politics of alternative culture, Verso, London, 1997

Fountain, Nigel: Underground, the London alternative press 1966-1974, Routledge, London, 1988

Frank, Thomas and Matt Weiland: Commodify your dissent, salvos from the Baffler, W. W. Norton, New York, 1997

Friedman, R. Seth: The Factsheet Five Zine Reader, the best writings from the underground world of zines, Three Rivers Press, New York, 1997

Goad, Jim: Answer Me! the first three, AK Press, San Francisco, 1996

Gore, Ariel: The Hip Mama Survival Guide, Hyperion Books, New York, 1998

Greenberger, David: Duplex Planet, Faber and Faber, Boston, 1994

Gunderloy, Mike and Cari Goldberg Janice: The World of zines, a guide to the independent magazine revolution, Penguin Books, London, 1992

Hoff, Al: Thrift Score, HarperCollins Publishers, New York, 1997

Holmstrom, John: Punk, the original, Trans-High Publishing, New York, 1996

Kelly, Jeff: Best of Temp Slave (Unabridged), Garrett County Press, New Orleans, 1997

Joliffe, Kira: Cheap Date, antidotal anti-fashion, Slab-O-Concrete, Hove, 2000

Kennedy, Pagan: 'Zine, how I spent six years of my life in the underground and finally...found myself...I think, St. Martin's Griffin, New York, 1995

Lukas, Paul: Inconspicuous consumption, the best of Beer Frame, Random House Value Publisher, New York, 1997

Mikul, Chris: Bizarrism, Headpress/Critical Vision, Manchester, 1999

Perry, Mark: Sniffin' Glue, the essential punk accessory, Sanctuary Publishing, London, 2000

Rowe, Chip: The book of zines, readings from the fringe, Henry Holt, New York, 1997

Sabin, Roger and Teal Triggs: Below Critical Radar, fanzines and alternative comics from 1976 to now, Slab-O-Concrete, Hove, 2001

Smith, Erica: The GirlFrenzy Millennial, the really big girl's annual, Slab-O-Concrete, Hove, 2000

Vague, Tom: The Great British Mistake, Vague 1977-1992, London, 1994

Vale, V.: Search and Destroy, no. 1-6, the complete reprint, V/Search, San Francisco, 1997

Vale, V.: Search and Destroy, no. 7-11, the complete reprint, V/Search, San Francisco, 1996

Vale, V.: Zines!, Vol. 1, V/Search, San Francisco, 1996

Vale, V.: Zines!, Vol. 2, V/Search, San Francisco, 1997